CW00969649

A Night in the Emperor's Garden

A Night in the Emperor's Garden

A True Story

Qais Akbar Omar

and

Stephen Landrigan

First published in 2011 by Haus Publishing Ltd as *Shakespeare in Kabul*

This expanded and updated edition published in 2015 by
Haus Publishing Ltd
70 Cadogan Place
London SW1X 9AH

A CIP catalogue record for this book is available from the British Library

ISBN 978-1-910376-12-6
eISBN 978-1-910376-20-1

Typeset in Arno by MacGuru Ltd
Printed in Spain

www.hauspublishing.com

for Elspeth Cochrane

and with hopes that peace will one day return to Afghanistan.

Contents

Authors' Note

A Night in the Emperor's Garden is an expanded and updated telling of the authors' earlier book *Shakespeare in Kabul*, which chronicled the efforts of Afghan actors to stage Shakespeare's *Love's Labour's Lost* in Kabul in 2005 in the Dari language. In the ten years since, much has happened in the actors' lives. *A Night in the Emperor's Garden* provides the details, and in so doing presents fresh aspects of Afghanistan's story that too often have been overlooked.

Naw Ruz. The New Day.

Kabul. March 2005.

The start of the new year in Afghanistan is called Naw Ruz, the New Day. It falls on the first day of spring, and arrives with a powerful sense of new beginnings.

Rarely has a Naw Ruz brought more optimism than in 1384, the year the foreigners called 2005. Six months earlier, Afghans had elected a president for the first time. Voter turnout had been massive, swelled by millions of women determined to assert themselves after years of suppression by the Taliban.

Kabul had become a point of convergence. For thirty years, vast waves of Afghans – no one knows how many – had fled the successive brutalities of Communist repression, a vicious civil war, and the theocratic dictatorship of the Taliban. Now they were coming back, unshakeably resolved to rebuild Afghanistan and return it to the serenity and prosperity it had known for most of the twentieth century. Driving them was a determination to leave the horrors of the past in the past and to make up for lost time.

Among them were professionals who had earned advanced degrees in their years away and brought with them technical skills, investment capital and, most importantly, an awareness of how life is lived elsewhere. They used their knowledge of modern telecommunications to connect the isolated villages of Afghanistan to each other and to the world beyond.

They set up radio stations. Music, banned by the Taliban, suddenly was everywhere. New songs by young musicians expressed

1

exuberant hopes and national pride. Masters of classical Afghan instruments like the *rabab*, the *dutar* and the *tambur* began performing publicly again. Even rockers and rappers had their place, reconfiguring ancient languages like Pashto, Dari, Uzbeki and Turkmeni into unexpected meters.

Television stations aired poetry programs on which Afghanistan's rich trove of mystical and epic verse was recited. Families gathered in front of their screens, entranced. Hearing their beloved poems again made them believe that the gentler days of the past truly were returning.

Nothing more exemplified the country's cultural renaissance than the rapidly developing film industry. One Afghan film, the internationally acclaimed *Osama*, had won the Caméra d'Or award at Cannes two years before in 2003. Dozens of other movies were being made and shown on the growing number of television networks that were giving Afghan writers, directors and actors opportunities to create programs. Among them were many women who courageously challenged norms just by appearing in films and on television. All over the country, companies of actors were forming and disbanding, envisioning projects, looking for money.

In Kabul, one clutch of actors had a chance meeting with an actress visiting from Paris for Naw Ruz. An idea took shape. None of their lives would ever be the same again.

This is their story.

A Night in the Emperor's Garden

A Gathering of Players

Kabul. March 2005.

Shah Mohammed was in the studio doing a voice-over for a radio commercial when he noticed Nabi Tanha waiting for him in the corridor. He looked at the clock as he started another take. He knew Nabi did not like to be kept waiting. As soon as he could, he popped his head out of the studio door, intending to tell Nabi that he would be finished in ten minutes. Nabi said curtly, "We have to go." He started walking away, expecting Shah Mohammed to follow.

"Where? I have another voice-over to finish," Shah Mohammed called after him.

"Do it tomorrow. We have to go to the Foundation for Culture and Civil Society."

"Today?" Shah Mohammed asked. "The actors' meeting is not until Thursday."

"Some French actress is coming this afternoon to meet actors. Qader Faroukh and his group will be there. We should go too. I don't want to miss out if she has a big project." Studio staff passing in the hall recognized Nabi, who was taller than most, and greeted him formally, placing their right hands over their hearts as a sign of respect. They asked about his health, family and work. Nabi politely answered them with the same questions, neither knowing who they were, nor waiting for their responses as he headed for the door.

Shah Mohammed ran back inside the studio and invented some excuse for having to leave during the recording session, then grabbed the U.S. Army jacket he always wore.

He found Nabi outside in the street, surrounded by a crowd who, until they spotted him, had other things to do. A girl dressed in a school uniform screamed, "Nabi, I want a picture with you," then suddenly felt shy and shrank back into the crowd. Her friends giggled and followed her.

"Nabi, I want your autograph," a teenager requested as he drew back his shoulders, "right here on my chest."

A slightly younger boy in muddy and torn clothes echoed him, yelling, "I want your autograph right here on my penis! Will you give it to me, Bulbul?"

The crowd shot the boy dirty looks.

"What are you looking at?" the boy protested with mock affront. "He's not going to sign that guy's chest either."

Nabi paid no attention to any of them as he mounted his red motorcycle. Shah Mohammed jumped on behind him. He was broader than Nabi. His mop of black hair was blown back by the wind. They lurched forward into the crowded roadway with a group of young boys running after them.

People in the cars were calling, "Bulbul, give my best to your wife, Gul Chera!" or "Nabi, I love you!" They completely ignored the heroic over-sized photos of President Hamid Karzai and the assassinated guerrilla leader Ahmad Shah Masoud that hung on the front of the nearby Municipality Building. Nabi acted like a deaf man and showed no reaction.

At the main intersection near Zarnegar Park, the head of the traffic police, who wore many medals on his chest, gave Nabi a salute as if he were the new president. Two other traffic policemen recognized Nabi and blew their whistles to open a lane for him to pass.

From there, Nabi and Shah Mohammed headed into the Da Afghanan district, where not even traffic police could untangle the cars, pedestrians, donkeys and pushcarts full of fruits and vegetables. Indeed, an ambulance with its siren blaring was caught in the

gridlock just like the rest. The drivers in the cars honked point-
lessly, competing with the shouts of the vendors on the sidewalks
and the loud music of the restaurants with their tacky sparkly light
bulbs.

Nabi usually loved driving through Da Afghanan. He enjoyed
all the attention he got in the traffic there. That day, however, he
was determined to be at the Foundation before Qader Faroukh
and his crew arrived. He wanted to be the first to meet the Frenchwoman and see why she was in Kabul. With so much foreign
money flowing into Afghanistan, maybe she had come with some
funding for a new project.

Nabi eased the motorcycle up onto the sidewalk and threaded
his way through the pedestrians until they reached Salang Watt,
one of Kabul's busiest streets. Shah Mohammed pulled off his
jacket and used it to cover his nose. He detested the stench of the
open sewers along the road.

Finally they reached the steep, rutted lane that led from Salang
Watt up to the Foundation. The narrow roadway was muddy from
the house drains that emptied into it. Several women in blue *burqas*
walked past, tightly gripping the hands of young boys or girls on
whose eyes they depended. With only small, netted openings in
the *burqas* to see through, the women were virtually blind. They
looked down at the road and carefully sidestepped the streams of
raw effluent.

Nabi maneuvered the motorcycle around the taxis and bicy-
cles, careful to avoid hitting the little kids racing all around them.
Halfway up, they saw their actor friend Faisal Azizi coming down
towards them.

"Hey, Ahmad Zahir!" Nabi shouted. Some of Faisal's friends
had told him that he looked like the famous Afghan pop singer. He
loved Ahmad Zahir's songs, and sang them all the time.

Faisal looked up and opened his arms wide. "What are you guys
doing here?" he asked with his permanent smile.

"Come to the Foundation with us."

"Today is not our Thursday meeting."

"There is a Frenchwoman who wants to meet some actors."

"Now?" Faisal was strong and well built, though not tall. At the mention of a woman, he stood a little straighter.

"Yes."

"I have to get some *naan* from the bakery for my family." After a few seconds, however, Faisal said, "Oh, let them chew wheat instead. Let's go and see this exotic Frenchwoman."

"Who said she was exotic?" Shah Mohammed asked.

"You can't stop a man from imagining things," Faisal said. He jumped on the motorbike behind Shah Mohammed for the brief ride back up the hill.

High mud-brick walls on either side of the lane gave no indication of what lay within. Only one door stood open. Above it hung a small sign that read "Foundation for Culture and Civil Society."

::::::

The wealthy family who owned this house was living elsewhere, renting their mansion to the *kharijees*, the foreigners, for large sums. In those post-9/11 days, Kabul was filling up with aid workers from dozens of countries. Landlords were charging huge rents to house them.

Most of the foreigners had come to Afghanistan knowing little about the country or its people. One notable exception was a Dutchman named Robert Kluijver. An adventurer, a scholar of Islamic culture and a multi-linguist who was fluent in Dari, Robert had come to Afghanistan in 2000 near the end of the Taliban era to set up programs for a European-financed charity, The Society for the Preservation of Afghanistan's Cultural Heritage. In 2003, he was named the director of the Foundation for Culture and Civil Society, one of the many new organizations in Kabul funded by foreign donors who believed that revitalizing the arts was essential to rebuilding Afghanistan.

Robert had sought out the large number of musicians, writers, and actors who were forming groups all over Kabul. He invited them to use the Foundation's large rooms for concerts, poetry readings or just as a space for talking over ideas. He set up a small library and frequently showed classic films from Europe and the United States as a way of generating discussions.

Nearly all those who came to the Foundation were men. They had spent years with their lives on hold, living in refugee camps in Iran and Pakistan or dodging rockets in Afghanistan. Now they were desperate to make up for lost time. Many came looking for training or advice; others, because they had nowhere else to go to meet those who shared their interests.

∷∷

Nabi parked the motorcycle just outside the Foundation's tall wooden door. Nearby, a small cemetery held a dozen graves marked by piles of stones and green flags fluttering in an early evening breeze. This place had once been far out in the country; the dead had expected to rest in peace. But the city had engulfed them, and now even a small flat area next to the graves was crammed with vendors selling phone cards, chewing gum, cold drinks and cigarettes from carts called *karachis*.

Nabi, Shah Mohammed and Faisal made their way through a dog-legged entry hall and into the large garden that filled the Foundation's central courtyard. It was a gentleman's garden, laid out a century and a half earlier, and nestled between the arms of a gracious mansion that embraced it on three sides. A high wall on the fourth side enclosed its carefully constructed landscape of terraces, balconies, niches and staircases.

They found Robert at his desk in a small office with a large window overlooking the garden. He had returned the night before from the northern Afghan city of Mazar-e-Sharif where he had staged a music and poetry festival to mark Naw Ruz. He was weary but happy to see them.

"How was your trip, Robert khan?" Nabi asked as he gave him a generous hug.

"I wish all of you had been there." Robert shook hands and kissed Shah Mohammed and Faisal on their right cheeks in the Afghan way of greeting among men. "We had Uzbeks and Turkmen and Pashtuns and Panjshiris playing music that has hardly been heard outside their villages for years," he said with deep satisfaction. "All these ethnic rivalries everyone talks about?" he asked rhetorically with a wave of his hand, "Nowhere to be seen. They were lost in the good feelings."

He told them about a presentation the night before the concert that he had organized in the Governor's Residence to celebrate the mystical Afghan poet Rumi. He had asked some Afghans to read Rumi's verses in Dari and the American poet Coleman Barks to read his translations in English.

In the audience was an actress from Paris named Corinne Jaber who had introduced herself to Robert afterward. Robert immediately invited her to come meet the actors at the Foundation after she returned to Kabul. "She can talk to you guys about what actors do in other countries."

"Has she made a lot of movies?" Nabi asked.

"I have no idea," Robert replied. "I met her only briefly. There she is." He nodded towards the garden. "You can ask her yourself."

Through the window, Shah Mohammed saw an attractive woman wearing a knee-length silk coat, a *chapan*, of a style worn in Mazar. A scarf with brightly colored stripes draped over her curly black hair that fell in masses around her face. She was talking with Qader Faroukh and his group of actors.

"Let's go meet her," said Robert as he led the way out of his office and down the steps to the garden.

She was shaking hands with the actors, all men, and introducing herself. "I am Corinne Jaber," she said in a rich throaty voice. Though she was then forty, she had the fitness of an athlete and the smooth, soft skin of a much younger woman. Her dark eyes were lively and engaging. Nabi, Shah Mohammed and Faisal added their welcomes when Robert introduced them.

"There are so many of you," she noted with approval, speaking to them with the help of a man in his early twenties who had arrived with her and was serving as her interpreter. "I didn't know Afghanistan had so many actors." Then she turned to Robert, "Do you have something that we can spread on the grass to sit on?"

"Of course," Robert replied. He spoke briefly to one of his staff then excused himself to go back to his office. A few minutes later, a large Hazaragi *kilim* was being carried out of one of the rooms and laid in the center of the lawn. The *kilim's* flat-woven oranges, reds and blues complemented the colors of the geraniums and tulips around the borders of the garden. It looked old. It had been made by women whose names would never be known, and who probably never thought of what they were weaving to cover their floor as the great art that it was.

Corinne sat at one end with the men in two lines facing one another, their shoes lined up neatly at the *kilim's* edge. The afternoon air was unusually soft. A couple of trees in the garden were in bloom and their delicate scent hung everywhere. Light slanted over the small, steep mountain that rose behind the Foundation.

Everyone was smiling at Corinne as she started telling them about her trip to Mazar and how intriguing she had found all the Afghan culture she had encountered, especially the poetry which she had heard quoted by people from all walks of life. After a few minutes, Faisal politely interrupted to ask, "Can you please tell us who you are and about your professional achievements?"

Corinne was not expecting such a direct question. It would be a while before she understood the Afghan way of speaking bluntly. Through the interpreter, Corinne told them about herself. "I have been an actress since I finished school. I worked for many years with a very well-known director named Peter Brook."

"I know about Peter Brook," an older actor named Kabir Rahimi interjected. Kabir was in his fifties. "I saw him when he came to Kabul in the 1970s to make a movie called *Meetings with Remarkable Men*. There were so many people to make one film. He was like a general, but very quiet."

Corinne nodded. "He's exceptional." She told them about how she had performed in Brook's production of the Indian epic *The*

Mahabharata. She had toured with it to several countries. Then she described how in Africa Brook and his troupe would arrive in a village, spread a carpet on the ground and just start performing. He called these performances "carpet shows."

"Since Afghanistan is filled with magnificent carpets," Corinne said, "perhaps you could do the same here."

"What movies have you made?" Nabi asked.

"Nearly all my work has been in the theater," she told them. She spoke with a self-assurance and warmth that made the actors feel comfortable with her. "A year ago, I received the Molière Award for acting in a play in Paris about the Armenian genocide. Maybe you've heard of that." Nobody had.

Then she asked about what they had done, especially in theater. A few of them had acted in some plays in the 1970s before the fighting had started. Most of their recent work, though, had been on television, or in the low-cost Dari- and Pashto-language video dramas that served up thrillers and sentimental stories to local viewers on DVDs.

"Afghans," Qader Faroukh explained, "have a relatively short theatrical tradition, if you don't count the theater that was built by Alexander of Macedon when his army occupied parts of Afghanistan." Everyone laughed. Alexander had led his army into what is now Afghanistan around 330 BCE. He left behind thousands of Macedonians and Greeks whose descendants still live there.

"In the far northeast of our country, he founded a city on the Amu Darya river to mark the farthest border of his empire. The buildings included a classical, open-air Greek theater. Parts of it remain in a place now called Ai Khanum. It is the easternmost Greek theater ever built."

"You know your history," Corinne noted approvingly.

"I'm older than all these young and talented actors," Qader Faroukh said graciously as he indicated the others seated on the *kilim.* He was dressed in a black suit and red tie. Everyone else was wearing jeans and shirts. "Not that I knew Alexander Sahib personally …" The others chuckled. "But I was trained at Kabul University before the civil war started."

"And I was, too," Nabi interjected, with a hint of (

Qader Faroukh ignored Nabi's interruption an
that theater in Afghanistan really started with tł
the performing arts program at Kabul University m ⌐

Nabi added, "We studied with teachers who had come from ɯ⌐
United States, Europe and Turkey. Some of my classmates went to
those countries for advanced training after they graduated."

One of the other actors told Corinne about the modern, fully-
equipped theater the Germans had built in Kabul in the 1970s.

"I can take you to it," Shah Mohammed offered. "People try to
put on shows there, but there are holes in the roof from the rockets
that hit it during the civil war – you can have a good view of the sky
while you watch the play."

Faisal mentioned how the Russians had established a modern
performing arts centre in the 1980s, when they were occupying
Kabul. "The Kabul police and fire departments had their own
theater companies when the Russians were here, and they put on
a lot of shows. It was a beautiful place. The shows were good. We
used to love it when our parents took us there." No more. After the
Soviets left in 1989, the Russian center suffered heavy damage and
subsequently became a wasteland haven for drug users.

The actors who had studied at Kabul University told Corinne
about the plays that they had done there by Aeschylus, Brecht,
Shakespeare, Molière and other foreign playwrights. They relished
the opportunity to talk about these writers after so many years
with so few opportunities to discuss them. Corinne was intrigued.
She had had no idea that classical plays like these had ever been
performed in Afghanistan.

Corinne suggested, "Let's do a series of movement exercises."

Everyone stood up. They all looked excited to have an opportunity to learn something new. Corinne led them in the stretches
and vocal exercises that actors in France did, then asked them to
impersonate animals. Nabi slunk into the crawl of a lion, as if he
had been raised in a pride. Qader Faroukh, without doing anything, projected raw animal power behind a façade of calculating

13

calm. A distinguished-looking middle-aged man with the gravitas of a prime minister and a deep voice to match, he was cast a few years later as a retired Afghan general in the film, *The Kite Runner*. He was well chosen for that part.

Kabir Rahimi impersonated something with wings. A bird? A butterfly? A bat? He affected an uncertain look as he sought somewhere to land, then total contentment as he settled on his perch. It was all precisely rendered with an economy of movement. Corinne was entranced.

Shah Mohammed threw himself into his improvisations as if he were engaged in hand-to-hand combat. He rolled on the ground, made big gestures, was wide-eyed one moment and terrifying the next. Adding to the illusion was the U.S. Army jacket that he was wearing; he had bought it in the Bush Market, named for the American president, where items that "fell off the trucks" heading to the American military bases were sold for almost nothing.

As the session wore on, Nabi's group of actors and Qader Faroukh's appeared to be competing. When Nabi looked displeased about something, everyone in his faction followed suit, even if they were not sure why. The same seemed to be true of the other group when Qader Faroukh appeared dismissive. Still, they absorbed every word that came from Corinne, "like a dry sponge in water" as Faisal said later.

After little more than an hour, however, everyone had to go home. Clouds had darkened the sky earlier than usual, and chill air was suddenly sliding off the mountain behind the Foundation, as happens at high altitudes such as Kabul. Someone had turned on the lights that ringed the garden. Birds recently arrived with the spring were flying from tree to tree, looking for places to roost.

As the session was ending, Nabi announced to Corinne, "If you were with us for six months, we could challenge the whole country." The other actors voiced their agreement.

Corinne told them that if they were interested in continuing what they had started, she would be happy to come back the following day. They all agreed, then lined up to have their photos taken with her, in groups and by themselves.

Everyone said their goodbyes, but before they left Corinne told the men, "Please bring some women tomorrow." She was determined not to let Taliban values prevail. There was a great silence. Finally, a few of the men said they would try as they headed out of the garden into the lane.

Everyone was in a hurry to get home. Shops were clanking down their metal shutters. Youngsters were running to nearby bakeries to buy fresh *naan* flat bread for their families' dinners. The muezzins in the mosques were calling for evening prayers. The air was filled with smoke, dust and the smell of sweat and open ditches. And possibilities.

A World of Possibilities

Kabul. March 2005.

Parwin Mushtahel was cooking rice, meatballs and *sabzi* for her family's evening meal when she received the call from Nabi Tanha.

After the usual formal greetings, he said, "I want to talk to you about something important, but I think you're busy. I can hear the sound of cooking."

"I can spare a few minutes."

"There is a woman from Paris at the Foundation. I went to see her this afternoon. She wants to meet some actresses."

"What for?"

"Maybe she has some kind of a project in mind. Maybe Robert does. Nobody has said. I told her that I'll find her a few actresses. I called you first. Can you come tomorrow afternoon?"

"I'll try. Thanks for thinking about me."

"There is no need to thank me, Parwin jan. You're like an older sister to me. You're always in my thoughts. I will let you go now so you don't burn what you're cooking. I can even smell it over the mobile. I'll see you tomorrow. God be with you."

"God be with you, Nabi jan," Parwin laughed.

Parwin carried the food into the living room where a large TV sat on a low table at the far end. The floor was covered with traditional Afghan red carpets. Photos of Parwin with her husband and their children enlivened the walls. Parwin had hidden her family's photos for the five years when the Taliban were in power. She had stitched some of them inside their mattresses and quilts to keep them safe.

Her husband Tawab sat cross-legged at the head of the eating cloth she had spread on the floor. Their four-year-old son Ahmad sat on his right and their daughter Shogufa, who was two years older, on his left. Parwin sat opposite Tawab. She and the children politely waited for Tawab to take the first bite. Then they followed his lead.

In quiet times like these, Parwin felt herself filled with the happiness that came from simple things. Her husband treated her and their children well. She knew that after they finished eating, he would ask the children what they had learned that day in their kindergarten.

They were not a wealthy family, but they had what they needed: two rooms and a small courtyard outside with a well in the center. A few small peach and apple trees grew along the wall near the gate. They rented the rooms from her sister and brother-in-law who owned the house and lived in another part of it.

After they had eaten, Parwin collected the dishes and took them to the well to wash them. Then she lit a fire in a very large samovar. An hour later, she poured the boiling water into buckets and tempered them with cold water before carrying them to the bathroom. She went to the living room where Tawab was playing with Ahmad and Shogufa and told him, "Everything is ready for your baths."

When Tawab had finished pouring one small bucket of warm water over his head after another, Parwin washed the children and then herself. Then all four of them went back to the living room and settled themselves in front of the television.

Before going to bed, Shogufa and Ahmad wanted to watch *Bulbul*. It was the first truly Afghan television series in the years since the Taliban. Bulbul was a former drug addict who had stopped smoking hashish and opium. He was now fighting the opium growers and encouraging boys and girls in his village to go to school. He had become a wise old man from whom everyone sought advice, except his wife, Gul Chera, who always nagged him.

Shogufa and Ahmad loved watching Bulbul because they had met him. Though Parwin had explained to them many times that they should call him Uncle Nabi, they still addressed him as Bulbul.

Parwin and Tawab had another reason for enjoying *Bulbul.* Two years earlier, Parwin had fulfilled a lifelong ambition of becoming an actress. She quickly found work making advertisements for television. Her first ad for a washing machine led to offers from many other companies who wanted her unaffected, maternal manner to help sell their products. Among the ads on *Bulbul* that evening were three featuring Parwin.

Tawab enjoyed watching his wife on TV. He was proud of her for being successful. After the Taliban had been toppled, he had encouraged her to chase her dream. She had auditioned for a few film companies, who all showed interest in her. That had increased her confidence enough for her to audition with the professors of the Kabul University Theater Faculty. They gave her a role in the first play produced at Kabul University after the Taliban. It was broadcast on national television and made Parwin famous overnight as the first woman to appear on Afghan television in a play. The television audience readily identified with her character, a woman who had lost everything in war and then gone mad.

Tawab had never told any of his relatives that his wife was acting. Neither television nor electricity had yet reached the rural areas where they lived. In his relatives' minds, it would be shameful for a woman to be seen on television, where men outside her family could look at her. In their village, a woman almost never left her home, and then only when accompanied by a male relative.

:::::

While they were watching *Bulbul,* someone knocked on the metal gate to their courtyard.

"Who could that be at this time of the night?" Tawab asked. His relatives from the countryside often came to spend the night when they needed to be in Kabul to do business or to see doctors. They showed up unexpectedly, though usually not so late. Perhaps it was one of them.

Parwin peered through the window and saw Tawab's older brother with his son. She hastily looked for her headscarf; her in-laws would expect her to have her head covered. Then she went through the DVDs among the pile near the TV, found one of the Bollywood actress Kareena Kapour and quickly slotted it into the TV. Ahmad and Shogufa protested that they wanted to watch the end of *Bulbul*.

"Get up and go to your beds," she said softly as she ushered them to their bedroom, saying, "We'll see *Bulbul* another night." She did not want her in-laws to catch sight of her on TV. If Tawab's brother did, he would share that news with the rest of the village and make things difficult for Tawab. It was always a big worry for her when they came to Kabul.

Parwin ran to the courtyard to welcome the visitors. Then she went to the kitchen to make them tea. They talked until midnight, with Kareena Kapour dancing and singing, and Parwin anxious that her in-laws would ask to switch to the local TV channel. Thank God they never did. They enjoyed watching Kareena Kapour too much, one minute in a Bollywood studio, and the next somewhere in Switzerland, Toronto or London.

∴∴∴

Parwin woke up before sunrise and did her morning prayers in her room. Her husband and in-laws did theirs in the courtyard. Then she lit the fire in the samovar to make tea. She woke up her daughter and son, dressed them, and ran back to the kitchen to prepare breakfast. As she chopped scallions into small pieces, she worried anew that someone might turn on the TV. She worked as quickly as she could, cutting up tomatoes before stir-frying them with the scallions into a dozen eggs. Then she took everything to the living room. Tawab had already spread the white cloth on the floor. Everyone was gathered around it, sipping their tea.

When they had finished eating, Tawab took his brother and nephew to the doctor, and Parwin released a long sigh of relief. Quickly, she put on the long brown skirt and black jacket that she wore to her job at the Afghan National Television station. She took Shogufa and Ahmad with her.

:·:·:·:

Across Kabul, Corinne was getting ready to go to the police station. Her passport had disappeared on her trip to Mazar. She would have to file a police report to obtain a replacement. She was always very careful about important things like passports, and was unnerved at having lost hers. She knew she had seen it in her purse when they had stopped for petrol outside Mazar, but after that ...

She went out onto the terrace of the old mud-brick fort with a cup of espresso to wait for the interpreter to come and help her with the police. He lived with his family in the rooms below. With his help, she had already gone to a few carpet shops and walked the old streets in Kabul.

She was relishing her time in the old fort. It was an impressive structure, built on the side of a low hill by a king as a residence for one of his chief advisors. On one side, its windows framed the towering, snow-covered Hindu Kush mountains to the north. On the other, a door led out to a second-story terrace that overlooked a courtyard full of roses, lilacs and a tall acacia tree. The friend with whom she was staying, David Elliot, had come to Kabul six months earlier and was reconstructing some of the larger rooms in exchange for their use. He had left early that morning for his job with an international organization.

While she sipped her coffee, she thought about the actors. Their enthusiasm, openness, sense of humor and, above all, their craving to learn had impressed her. The way they spoke had a kind of poetry to it. In fact, poetry seemed to permeate everything she had experienced in Afghanistan.

She thought about her trip to Mazar. David had arranged for

the two of them to travel with a group of Sufis who were making a pilgrimage to the shrine in Mazar of Hazrat Ali, the cousin and son-in-law of the Prophet Mohammed, peace be upon him. As they had driven north from Kabul, the Sufis had recited the classical Persian poets for hours upon end; when one stopped, another started.

Though she could not understand the language, she could hear the cadences in the words and the passion in their voices. In Mazar, she and David had gone at night to see the domed blue-tiled shrine, its minarets and niches aglow with strings of lights. Inside the shrine, Afghans who had come from all over the country were paying their respects at the elaborately decorated, bejeweled tomb. They brushed it with brightly-colored paisley scarves in the hope of taking the blessings of the holy place home with them. Swirling calligraphy was everywhere, transforming words into art.

On Naw Ruz itself, she and David had traveled nine miles west to Balkh to see what was left of the world where the poet Rumi had been born eight hundred years ago. He and his family had been forced to flee by the onslaught of Genghis Khan. The refugee story in Afghanistan, it seemed to Corinne, was never-ending.

She sat on a low wall at the edge of the old fort's terrace and thought about the massive thousand-year-old walls she had seen at Balkh. And of the remains of fourteenth-century arches from the age of Tamburlaine that soared within. And of the women in white *burqas* she had seen streaming to the grave of a young woman poet from the fifteenth century, Rabia Balkhi, who died for love. Their *burqas* billowed out behind them as they walked. Mysteriously, a large white owl had swooped from the top of the shrine, though it was midday.

Nearby, a large group of men had gathered in a circle to dance the *atan*, a Pashtun warrior's dance, propelled by the pounding of deep-throated drums. A goat kicked up its heels dancing alongside them.

The images kept racing through her mind, hints of a rich culture she knew nothing about. Then there were the Kuchi nomads she had seen on the drive back to Kabul and their black goat-hair tents pitched alongside a river. Unaccompanied Kuchi girls dressed in colorful outfits walked between the tents and the river to draw water in pots they carried on their heads.

Their life as nomads was obviously harsh, but they were clearly freer than other Afghan women such as those in the Sufi family where she and David had spent a night. She had been shunted off to the women's quarters, leaving her feeling isolated and resentful. A few days later when David was invited to a Sufi religious ceremony, a *zikkur*, Corinne was not. Women never are.

There were things about Afghanistan that Corinne did not like. Yet everything she was experiencing made her hungry to know more.

She heard the interpreter closing the door of his family's rooms below and coming up the steps in the small tower at one end of the terrace. She finished her coffee and felt as if the process of making sense of her experiences had only just begun. And then there was Nabi Tanha's proclamation the day before: "If you were with us for six months, we could challenge the whole country." She had to leave in two days, if she got her new passport. But what if she could come back?

"Are you ready?" the interpreter asked.

::::::

When Nabi and Shah Mohammed came into the Foundation's garden later that afternoon, Parwin Mushtahel was already there, seated on a bench. Her two children were running around on the grass. Short and matronly, Parwin's large curls of auburn hair constantly fought to dislodge her headscarf. She maintained both the headscarf and an air of quiet dignity.

Several of the actors who had been there the day before were standing around, along with others whom Nabi had called. Strangely, neither Qader Faroukh nor any of his group were present. Faisal came sidling in after a few minutes, singing. Behind him was Corinne.

From the moment she arrived, Corinne took charge. She strode into the garden and walked to the center of the Hazargi *kilim*, which awaited them on the lawn, and invited the actors to gather in a circle. She had devised a series of activities, she told them as they settled around her. Her years of projecting her lines to upper balconies had endowed her with a voice that commanded attention.

Nabi introduced her to Parwin. Corinne said she was grateful to meet her, but disappointed that Parwin was the only woman who had come.

It was a raw day, not like the balmy afternoon before. Corinne and the actors worked together for more than an hour in a chill wind. She led them through some physical and vocal exercises different from those of the day before. The exercises were followed by more improvisations. Nabi volunteered to play the moon, and he asked the other actors to play the stars. An Afghan who worked at the Foundation paused to watch them as he made his way to his office. It was clear from the look on his face that he could make no sense of what was going on. The actors, though, were having a good time stretching their imaginations.

After a while, tea came out to the garden on large trays. Nothing can be done in Afghanistan without green tea. The *kilim* was transformed from a stage to a *chai khana*, a teahouse. While they were busying themselves with the cakes and cookies that had come with the tea, Qader Faroukh appeared.

He went directly to Corinne and, after lengthy formal greetings, explained that "My group and I won't be able to participate further with you. I'm very sorry for that. But I'm happy because today I signed a big contract to do a series of short plays about democracy all over Afghanistan. I must get the plays up and running in less time than I need. I have come to ask your permission to be excused from your sessions." He pressed his right hand to his chest.

"It is very kind of you to come and tell me in person," Corinne said. "Good luck with your project. I hope we have a chance to work together in the future."

"I'd like that very much."

When Nabi saw Qader Faroukh leave and learned why, a victorious smile spread across his face.

After fifteen minutes, Corinne asked everyone to finish their tea so they could continue working. Discussions that begin over a cup of tea, however, can go on for days. None of the actors paid attention until Nabi happened to glance at Corinne and perceived her eagerness to get started again. He clapped his hands authoritatively, and said in a loud voice, "Stop eating and drinking and chattering. Let's work!"

Immediately, everyone put down their tea and half-nibbled cookies.

:::::

For the rest of the afternoon, Corinne wanted to see if it was possible to harness the creativity of the random improvisations they had done earlier. She asked the actors to improvise the scene from *A Midsummer Night's Dream* in which workmen enact the ancient Greek story of Pyramus and Thisbe. Corinne outlined the basic plot of the long-told tale of forbidden love. Then she asked them to act out the scene, and to improvise as they went.

The result was astonishing. To start with, the men had no hesitation in playing the female parts. The elderly actor Kabir covered his head with a scarf to become the young girl Thisbe. Another actor took on the role of the wall, and with his thumbs and forefingers formed a chink through which the pining lovers could speak. All of them showed an unhesitating readiness to get up and tell a story.

To keep the gender-bending balanced, Corinne asked Parwin to play a man. Without a pause, she exchanged her headscarf for one of the men's flat woolen *pakhol* hats and wrapped herself in a *patu*, a woolen shawl worn by men. When she spoke, she did so in a gruff, deep voice.

The actors performed with enthusiasm. Then they repeated the scene, with each actor taking a different role. Some of them had never heard of Shakespeare, but they all agreed that he had come up with an excellent story.

::::

Much too soon for all of them, the afternoon slipped into evening. "I have to go home," Parwin said apologetically. "It is getting late and I won't be able to find a taxi. Nabi will tell me what you are planning to do next."

"I don't know what is next," Corinne said.

All the actors frowned.

"We should make a movie," Shah Mohammed said.

"Maybe," Corinne said. "Maybe not. Perhaps a play."

Robert Kluijver had told her during the tea break that he was eager to have her return and do something large-scale. But what? More workshops? A series of scenes? A full play? The task was to find the right project that could be meaningful to these actors, both personally and professionally.

The actors left for their homes, all expressing the wish that Corinne would come back and work with them. The next day, temporary passport in hand, Corinne left for Paris, her imagination whirling.

Selecting a Play

Paris. April 2005.

Back in Paris, with the dust of Kabul in her shoes, Corinne thought at length about the actors she had met and Robert Kluijver's proposal that she return to Afghanistan and work with them. If she did go, she would have to juggle family obligations and some work commitments. She might just be able to do that. But to do what in Kabul?

Anything less than a full production of a play made no sense, she concluded. If she could take the actors from a first reading to a closing night, she could expose them to a range of experiences that would serve them well in the future.

Within days, she met the noted French theater director Ariane Mnouchkine, who has worked with theater artists from around the world. She had already been enlisted by Robert to do workshops in Kabul that summer with young Afghan actors. These would be part of a larger Afghan Theater Festival that Robert was organizing.

Corinne and Ariane talked at length about what sort of play made sense for Afghan actors. They agreed that the tradition of epic poetry in Afghanistan pointed towards one of the great poet-playwrights. Ariane suggested *Tartuffe*, by Molière. Its exploration of greed made it unwittingly prescient of the corruption then beginning to exert its crippling stranglehold on Afghanistan.

Corinne wanted a play that called on the physical and emotional energy that she had seen the actors produce. She felt that *Tartuffe* lacked the force of Shakespeare. In her spacious, sky-lighted loft in an old industrial building near the Père Lachaise cemetery, she started thumbing through Shakespeare's plays. Foremost in her mind was finding one that had good parts for women. In so many of his plays, women have only minor roles. And in plays where women are major characters – Lady Macbeth, for instance – there are few other prominent female parts.

Some of the comedies have lots of good parts for women. However, Shakespeare has those women engage in male-female courtship rituals that would be problematic to stage in Afghanistan. Even with the Taliban gone, women faced limits on what they could do in public. Just having women on stage with men would be testing the boundaries.

There was one comedy, though, that caught her attention: *Love's Labour's Lost*. It is not so well known nor frequently produced, but it has four strong roles for women. Like many of Shakespeare's comedies, it is actually two plays in one. One is lowbrow, raunchy and full of topical references that no one since the play's premiere in the 1590s has understood without footnotes, except possibly some English majors. And then there is the second play, a kind of morality play enacted by four men and four women who bear titles of nobility. They speak some of the richest verse Shakespeare wrote. Their jokes evolve from within the play itself, and hence never feel dated.

The play starts with a haunting echo of the Taliban: the men vow to refrain from having any contact with women for three years. They will instead study and improve themselves spiritually. One of them, a king, issues an order that "no woman shall come within a mile of my court ... on pain of losing her tongue."

Almost immediately, four attractive young ladies from a neighboring kingdom arrive. What to do? Just as in Afghanistan, deeply-rooted customs require that the visitors be offered hospitality. The king cannot invite them into his palace without breaking the vow he and his friends have just made. Instead, he suggests that the ladies stay in a tent in the palace's garden. The ladies respond to this rather ridiculous situation with twinkles in their eyes and accept.

27

Soon, the men's hunger for the women overtakes their commitment to their vows. Each of them secretly sends a love letter to his favorite among the ladies, but without wanting the other men to know. This being Shakespearean comedy, the messenger entrusted with delivering the letters gives them to the wrong ladies. Before long, each of the young men discovers what the others have been doing. They decide that love is more spiritual than anything they might have studied, and set off to visit the women and express their true feelings. But in disguise.

What follows is as predictable as it is hilarious. The women hear about the men's plan, and disguise themselves as well. The men arrive but now each of them is wooing the wrong lady. This discovery leads to utter embarrassment among the men, who feel compelled to make a full confession of their true intentions.

The men want to be wed immediately. The women insist on a year's delay: if the men are still in love with them after one year of chastity and reflection, they will marry them. For the women of *Love's Labour's Lost*, the bride price they are demanding is total commitment on the part of the men.

So the play ends where it started, with the four young men going on a retreat. Now, however, their motives have changed, and are much more genuine. And importantly for Corinne, it is the women who decide the outcome, and impose conditions that the four young men accept.

This was exactly the kind of play that Corinne was looking for. Indeed it almost seemed that it had been written to be performed in the garden of the Foundation, with a Kuchi nomad tent set amid the rose bushes and pomegranate trees. She read the play several more times. By doing only the scenes that involved the nobles, she would have a tight drama that would run well under two hours. That would be more than enough for actors without recent experience of doing theater.

One nagging issue worried her, even as her confidence in *Love's Labour's Lost* grew. She had seen no actresses apart from Parwin. Were there others? What could they do?

In Kabul, Nabi's mobile kept ringing and interrupting him as he edited the last episode of *Bulbul*. All the actors who had met Corinne wanted to know when she would come back. He had no idea what to tell them. He called the interpreter, who was keeping in touch with Corrine via email. None of the actors then had access to the internet. The interpreter told them he had asked Corinne several times what her plans were. She had not given him any clear answer.

"We have to do something," Shah Mohammed said to Nabi, who was sitting beside him on a squeaky chair in the small, dark editing room. The screen of the computer illuminated their desk. "If Corinne isn't coming back, maybe we should just do something ourselves."

Nabi was focused on getting an edit just right. Shah Mohammed continued.

"Maybe we should get the other guys together and make a movie."

"How?" Nabi asked. "We need money."

"We can go to an embassy or a foreign organization and ask for some. If we have a good project, they'll fund us. They're giving money for all these other movies."

"We're actors, not producers."

"Saba Sahar is an actor *and* a producer," Shah Mohammed replied.

Nabi nodded. He did not say anything for a few minutes. "Maybe she knows something," he said suddenly. "Let's go ask her."

Minutes later, they were on Nabi's motorcycle, ignoring the people who yelled at him asking about the next episode of *Bulbul*.

Nabi and Shah Mohammed saw the "Saba Film" sign from far away. Written in white on a large piece of black cloth, it hung from the third floor balcony of a building that was painted yellow. The gentle breeze was making the sign wave like a flag.

Nabi parked his motorcycle at the side of the busy road. He and Shah Mohammed climbed the stairs to the third floor. There, a short man standing in front of a red door said softly, "They are recording. You cannot go in now." As soon as he recognized Nabi, though, he smiled and quietly opened the door, and gestured for them to walk inside.

Shah Mohammed and Nabi tried not to make any sound as they stood in a corner of what looked like a nicely decorated living room. There was a large red carpet on the floor with pillows arranged around it. Two actors were sitting on the carpet, one much older than the younger. In front of the older man was a dish full of money and a handgun. Saba was standing behind a large camera on a tripod. Two men with headsets were sitting on chairs on either side of her.

"Action," Saba instructed. She was wearing jeans with a red blouse. Her face showed her fondness for makeup; her eyelashes were thickened by mascara, and her eyelids were adorned with sparkling, blue eye shadow. A turquoise headscarf draped from her neck.

The younger man began sobbing.

"Cut," Saba said.

The eighteen-year-old boy cleared his tears with the back of his hand and smiled at Saba. The makeup artist ran from a corner of the room. She cleaned up the black *kohl* that ran under the young man's left eye, and added some more.

"As soon as he cries," Saba said to the older man, "you are supposed to pick up the gun and wave it around."

"All right," said the man, who appeared to be in his fifties. He had a narrow gray mustache, and was dressed in a white *shalwar kameez* and brown turban. His eyes were also blackened with *kohl*, which made him look like a thug.

"Three, two, one, action!"

The boy in a blue *shalwar kameez* starting crying again, and the old man did as he had been told.

"Cut," Saba said. The two men looked at Saba. "It doesn't look right. Instead of picking up the gun, you have to slap him."

"I don't want to be slapped," the young man protested as the makeup artist again fixed his *kohl*.

"If you don't want to do what I'm telling you, take off your costume. I don't have time to waste."

"All right. I will do it."

Saba stood behind the camera again and anxiously watched the scene. She was thirty-six years old. The first female Afghan film director and producer, she had set up her production company soon after the Taliban collapsed. Most of her movies were police dramas, with stories drawn from her other profession as a high-ranking officer in the Ministry of the Interior. She always took the part of the heroine herself: a female officer standing up for justice; a woman who did kung fu high kicks and rode a motorbike with no hands while firing a gun. As soon as her movies were released, everyone wanted to see them. She had become a household name across Afghanistan.

When the scene was done, Saba smiled while the young man rubbed his cheek and looked resentfully at the older actor who had slapped him. She had achieved what she wanted. "Good job, everyone!" she said. "We'll take a fifteen-minute break. I want everybody on set by quarter past three." Everyone walked out of the room. When Saba turned around, she noticed Nabi and Shah Mohammed. "What are you guys doing here?" she asked with surprise in her voice.

"We came to say hello," Nabi said.

"Very kind of you. Please follow me," she said as she walked to her office. There was a large shiny brown table with a black leather chair behind it. Books and papers were piled on her desk. She sat in her chair and took a deep breath. "It has been a long day. When you have to work with inept actors, life can be exhausting."

"I didn't recognize either of them," Shah Mohammed commented as he sat next to Nabi on a cream-colored couch in front of Saba's desk. "Why don't you get some professional actors and stop stressing yourself?"

"I want to bring new talents into the movie industry. Sometimes you hire so-called 'professionals,' and when you tell them to do something a certain way, they argue. At least these amateurs don't question me, but they are not easy to work with. Forget about me. Why are you guys here?"

Nabi cleared his throat. "Have you heard of this woman named Corinne who was in Kabul a couple of weeks ago?"

"She is some kind of French director, right?"

"No, she has never directed before," Shah Mohammed said. "She told us that she acted in some plays, and worked with Peter Brook." Saba nodded at Peter Brook's name.

"We hope she is going to do a project," Nabi said. "Shah Mohammed and I thought that maybe we should do something ourselves. Maybe get some funds from the Americans or some organization. We thought we should talk to you first. You know how these things work. You have one movie deal after another. Maybe we can work together to get some funds?"

Saba called the short man who was standing behind her office door and asked him to bring tea for her guests. Then she looked at Nabi and Shah Mohammed. "It is very kind of you, Nabi jan, to think of me. However, I have two movie projects with deadlines, and I'm way behind. At the moment, I can't commit to more projects."

Nabi smiled. "I'm glad to hear you have lots of work," he said.

"Talk to Robert at the Foundation," Saba said. "He knows who has money for movie projects more than I do. When I get busy with my films, I try not to think about what I have to do next. Distraction is not good for me. Maybe we can talk again in three months."

Nabi rose. "It was great seeing you after so long," he said. "Let me know if there is anything I can do to help."

"But you haven't had your tea yet," Saba said.

"It's fine," Nabi said. "You need to get back to work." He left the room in a rush, as if he were angry with Saba.

"I have to go too," Shah Mohammed said apologetically as he ran out of the room after Nabi.

Saba watched them go, and made a note to contact Robert at the Foundation to find out what Corinne was planning. She was a busy woman, yet she did not want to miss out on what sounded like what might be an interesting opportunity.

Making the Script

Kabul. May and June 2005.

As the idea of doing *Love's Labour's Lost* in Kabul was taking hold in Corinne's mind, questions swirled. She had never done anything as big as this, nor in a language she did not speak. Yet working across linguistic and cultural barriers did not faze her.

She had been born in Munich to a German mother and a Kurdish Syrian father, and had grown up amid a swirl of languages. For several years her family lived in Canada, where she mastered English. Later they returned to Germany. At eighteen, she took herself to Paris, learned French, and became an actress. She soon found herself at Les Bouffes du Nord working with Peter Brook and a company of actors from nearly every part of the world. What she was proposing to do in Kabul was in many ways just an extension of her existing life and work.

After she had been home for two weeks, she phoned Robert Kluijver and proposed doing a Shakespeare play, possibly *Love's Labour's Lost*. He loved the idea and asked if she could do it late in the summer.

It was already April. She would have to be home in Paris by early September to get her two teenage daughters started in the new school year. That left only five months to shape a script, get it translated into Dari, find a cast, make costumes, rehearse and all the rest. It would be tight, even working with a group of practiced professionals.

She read and reread some lines by a character in *Love's Labour's Lost* named Biron who is both the most poetic of the four young men in the play, and the most grounded. He makes an impassioned speech on the folly of forswearing the company of women:

> *From women's eyes this doctrine I derive;*
> *They are the ground, the books, the academes*
> *From whence doth spring the true Promethean fire […]*
> *For where is any author in the world*
> *Teaches such beauty as a woman's eye? […]*
> *But love, first learned in a lady's eyes,*
> *Lives not alone immured in the brain;*
> *But, with the motion of all elements,*
> *Courses as swift as thought in every power,*
> *And gives to every power a double power,*
> *Above their functions and their offices. […]*
> *From women's eyes this doctrine I derive:*
> *They sparkle still the right Promethean fire;*
> *They are the books, the arts, the academes,*
> *That show, contain and nourish all the world.*

"From women's eyes …" The words kept echoing in Corinne's mind. "From women's eyes …" She heard them as nothing less than a hymn to women. And they set in motion events that lead to a resolution decided by women. The words were powerful. And she believed strongly that they needed to be heard in Kabul.

:::::

With all this turning in her mind, Corinne decided that she needed to get back to Kabul as soon as possible, if only to find out whether the actors actually wanted to do *Love's Labour's Lost*. There was no point in staging a play that held no interest for them.

Skype was beginning to be widely used that year. With the help of its cost-free phone links, Corinne was able to stay in touch with an American playwright living in Kabul working with an international aid project. They had met at Naw Ruz in Mazar. She enlisted him to craft a script out of Shakespeare's.

"Disregard all the subplots, and the puns, and all that stuff," she shouted to the writer through an echo on the line. "Just focus on the four noblemen and the four noblewomen. There is a very good play in there."

Although she remained open to looking at other plays, she felt that if the actors could read a script of *Love's Labour's Lost* in Dari, they would want to do it as much as she did.

Over the next two weeks, some of Shakespeare's finest verse shuttled back and forth between Kabul and Paris. A tightly-structured script began to take shape with about 1,000 lines out of the original 2,785.

The next task was to get it translated into Dari.

∷∷∵

Shortly after Naw Ruz, the Kabul newspapers had carried the announcement of the death in Iran of Dr. Alaeddin Pazargadi at the age of ninety-five. A noted educator in Tehran, he had lived and taught for many years in England. There he had fallen in love with Shakespeare's poetry. An accomplished poet himself, he set himself the task of translating all of Shakespeare's comedies and tragedies into Farsi, the language of Iran. It had taken him the better part of fifty years to do so.

Dari is an older version of Farsi with many common words. Crafting a Dari version of the play based on Dr. Pazargadi's translation would be faster than commissioning a translation from English.

Kabul is a city of bookstores. The search began. Shah's Book Store, the subject of the much fictionalized bestseller, *The Bookseller of Kabul* by Åsne Seierstad, primarily stocks books in English. The owner said he would be happy to order a copy of Dr. Pazargadi's translation from Tehran, but it would be hard to know when it would come. Certainly not soon.

The local Dari and Pashto bookstores in Kabul's Shahr-e-Naw shopping district were full of gilt-edged editions of the poetry of Omar Khayyam and Hafez, but had no volumes of Shakespeare, in any language. In the open-air book bazaar in Deh Mazang, none of the bookselling squatters who had set up dozens of kiosks there had anything by Dr. Pazargadi, let alone Shakespeare.

:::::

While the search for the script was ongoing, Robert was raising funds. From the Germans, he received $3,000 through the Goethe-Institut. Then the British Council, the cultural affairs arm of the British Foreign Office, contributed $20,000. Even better, the British Council office in Tehran could send a photocopy of Dr. Pazargadi's translation of *Love's Labour's Lost* to the British Council in Kabul. Unfortunately, it had to travel via a slow-moving diplomatic pouch first to London, then to Kabul, taking nearly a month to make the journey.

:::::

A young Afghan, Qaseem Elmi, was given the task of preparing the Dari script. Qaseem was a natural linguist. The son of a Pashtun father and a Tajik mother, he had learned both Pashto and Dari as a toddler. After his family was forced to flee to a refugee camp in Pakistan when he was five, he had quickly picked up Urdu and mastered enough Arabic to read the Holy Koran. As a teenager, he realized that those with English language skills got better-paying jobs. He enrolled in English classes and soon was fluent.

Yet for all of that, Qaseem could not make sense of the Farsi in Dr. Pazargadi's translation. His first reaction on seeing it was to ask, "Which language is this?"

"Farsi," he was told. He looked at it again. Like most Dari-speakers, he could read and speak Farsi.

"Are you sure?" Then he picked up an English version of the play and read a few pages. Qaseem's brow furrowed. He took off his glasses. Without them, he bore a striking resemblance to the young Elvis Presley. He looked around, then put the glasses back on and looked again at the script.

"What kind of English is this?" he asked. He had never heard of Shakespeare.

:::::

Qaseem decided to have a typist enter Dr. Pazargadi's text into a Farsi/Dari word processing program.

The typist took days and extra days, as Afghans say, because whole sections of the photocopy had not reproduced well, and the print was tiny to start with. Plus, there were all those unfamiliar words. Adding further complication, the written versions of Farsi and Dari do not express all the vowel sounds of the spoken languages. Thus, a reader encountering an unfamiliar word for the first time must become a kind of detective to figure out its meaning. Several words like that in a single line would stop all progress as Qaseem and the typist puzzled over them.

What was becoming evident to Qaseem was that Dr. Pazargadi had used many archaic Farsi words to make the vocabulary of his translation as contemporaneous with Shakespeare's original language as possible. As a literary achievement, it was a milestone. As a script for a group of actors in Kabul, it was a massive challenge.

Qaseem called on the help of a colleague, Khan Mohammed Stanekzai, a highly accomplished Pashto poet who was also fluent in Dari. His poetic sensibilities helped unravel many of the linguistic riddles that Dr. Pazargadi had unintentionally concocted. Stanekzai would stand in Qaseem's office with his head tilted to one side as he gazed at the ceiling. Short and slim with an untamed thatch of curly hair, his lips would move silently as he repeated the lines that Qaseem had just read to him. Slowly he would work his way through the conundrum they presented, and start speaking as if he were channeling Shakespeare or Dr. Pazargadi.

How many words could they alter before the rhythms of Dr. Pazargadi's verse were lost or the clarity of Shakespeare's language became clouded? It was a delicate task. Stanekzai argued that at least half of the script should be translated into Pashto, since it was one of the national languages of Afghanistan, and more people speak it than Dari. As a poet, he said, he could ensure that the meters and subtleties of both Dr. Pazargadi's and Shakespeare's intentions were respected.

It was an intriguing notion. Might some of the characters speak in Pashto, and others respond to them in Dari? That kind of linguistic ping-pong happened every day on the streets of Kabul.

The issue was settled by the software in the computer. It could not easily mix the Dari and Pashto alphabets. Both are based on the Arabic alphabet, but Pashto has more letters and requires diacritical marks that Dari does not use. Just as well, since Qaseem and the typist were slowly going mad working only in Dari.

In retrospect, it was probably an error not to include more Pashto. The new Afghanistan would have to move beyond the ethnic fault lines of the past. Perhaps a deliberately multilingual script would have helped point the way.

::::

When the time came for Qaseem to put the Dari and English texts side by side, and delete the lines that had been cut in English, a new problem arose. In Farsi and Dari, verbs typically are placed at the end of the sentence. Shakespeare places his verbs where he needs them to support the meter or to lend poetic grace.

Qaseem worked tirelessly to sort all that out. He had a Farsi dictionary on one side of his desk and an English dictionary on the other. Frequently, he failed to find the sixteenth century words he sought in either. The word "duke," which Dr. Pazargadi used frequently, puzzled everybody working on the script. They could not find it in any Farsi dictionary. Then, somebody suggested that Qaseem look for it in an English dictionary – and there it was.

As the translation process wore on, Qaseem's friends started spending hours each day helping him. When they needed a break, Qaseem would arm-wrestle for a while with one of them. Once, in the middle of wrestling, he suddenly understood the meaning of a phrase that had been confusing everyone all afternoon. He was so excited that he relaxed his grip for a moment, allowing his opponent to slam his arm down on the table. He cried foul. But in Afghanistan, there are no excuses, only winners.

Discussions – conducted in three languages simultaneously – sometimes became heated. From time to time, one or another of them would walk out of the office, fed up. No Afghan can stay out of a good fight for long, however. A few minutes later, a cup of green tea in hand, he would come back in, determined to prevail.

Finally, the Dari version of the script was completed. One by one, the pages came out of the printer, each of them looking like small masterpieces of calligraphy.

Casting the Boys

Kabul. May 2005.

Before she left Paris to return to Kabul, Corinne called on Peter Brook. She wanted to ask his advice on directing Shakespeare in a place like Kabul. The man who had dazzled and challenged the English-speaking theater world throughout the second half of the twentieth century spoke to her in his soft voice. His message was simple. "Do not to impose your ideas on the Afghans. Listen to the actors and take what they have to give you."

It seemed like straightforward advice, but she had no way of knowing then just how hard it would be to follow, nor how much the Afghan actors had to give her.

:::::

Aref Bahunar walked across the campus of Kabul University heading for a pushcart along the main road in front of his dormitory. It was midday, and he wanted to buy some fried potatoes and an Afghan hamburger wrapped in a thin *naan* with cucumber, parsley, onion and tomatoes. All morning, he and his acting classmates had been doing physical exercises to learn how to move forcefully in a small space.

He joked with the vendor about the hungry dog lying nearby, desperately waiting for somebody to drop some food on the dusty street. Some days he felt like that himself. Then he went and sat on a bench in front of the Fine Arts Faculty of the Theater Department where he was studying.

He took a bite. It was not like the delicious meals his mother cooked back home in Ghazni province. Nothing in Kabul was as good. Instead of living in his family's compound, he was crowded into one room of a large dormitory at the university with several other students. Water was unpredictable, and electricity rare. At night when they needed to study, they would sit in clumps under the street lamps, reading.

When the memories of home came flooding in and threatened to make him sad, Aref distracted himself by studying harder. His goal was not to be comfortable, but to learn. He wanted his family to see him on the screen of their TV at home one day, and tell the other villagers that he was their son.

While he was eating, two of his classmates came and joined him. One of them ate some of Aref's potatoes. "I heard there is somebody doing some kind of a play or movie at the Foundation for Culture and Civil Society, someone else besides Ariane Mnouchkine," he said.

"Who?" Aref asked.

"I don't know. She was here just after Naw Ruz," his classmate replied. "One of Nabi Tanha's group of actors told me about her."

"You mean Bulbul?" Aref asked enthusiastically.

"Yes."

"We should join them," Aref said as he finished his hamburger and wiped his hands with a paper napkin.

"Getting into Nabi's group isn't easy," said the other classmate. "He already has a lot of actors."

Aref was not listening. In his mind, he was already at the Foundation asking who this person was.

:·:·:·:

Corinne arrived back in Kabul eager to get started. As she prepared to deplane, she slipped on a headscarf, as did the other women, mostly Western, who were not already covered. Just a few months ago on her first visit, having to wear a scarf had annoyed her. It still did, but her mind was on too many more important things to give it much attention.

The old fort had a feeling of familiarity when she stepped out of the car that brought her from the airport.

The next day, Corinne set up operations in a room at the Foundation that had once been a grand salon. It had tall windows that overlooked the garden. The same *kilim* on which she and the actors had sat on the lawn on her first visit now covered the floor.

About a dozen actors showed up on her first day there. As before, they were all men. Many were regular participants in the programs run by the Foundation, such as Nabi, Shah Mohammed and Faisal, but there were also several new faces that Corinne did not recognize. They were excited to be doing a project, even though they had no idea what it was. It really did not make much difference to them what they did; they just wanted to perform.

The actors sat down on the *toshaks*, floor cushions, that ringed the old *kilim*, and waited as green tea was brought for everyone. While cups were being filled and passed around, Corinne told them that she wanted to do a play by Shakespeare. She explained who he was and why his plays were still important four hundred years after he had written them.

Her deep voice filled the grand salon in a way that had the actors listening very carefully, even though most did not understand English. They had to wait for the interpreter to translate what she had said. She was careful not to mention *Love's Labour's Lost* by name. She had to be ready to do a different play in case she could not find enough actresses. Robert insisted that there were many others around Kabul. A couple of times he had specifically mentioned a young girl named Marina Golbahari, who had starred in the film *Osama*. Corinne had met only Parwin.

Without explaining why she was doing it, she then guided them through some improvisations based on the story of the four men in *Love's Labour's Lost*. She would explain a scene, and then have them play it in different ways. It gave her a chance to see who could do what. The actors were excited and responded enthusiastically to anything she suggested.

One set of actors played the men as princes. Another group acted more like university professors. When it was time for Nabi, Shah Mohammed and Faisal to have a turn, they and one of their friends decided to play them as Taliban. Corinne, like many foreigners at that time, had the impression that the Taliban were deeply religious men, even if they had some strange ways of expressing their piety. The actors, however, presented them from an Afghan perspective.

Nabi asked one of the actors if he could borrow his large, cotton neck scarf. He wrapped it around his head like a turban and sat in the center of the room. Faisal rolled up his trousers to his knees, revealing hairy legs. Shah Mohammed disheveled his finely combed hair, put on a white hat and sat next to Faisal.

"What is today's agenda?" Nabi asked, naturally assuming that he was the Taliban leader.

Shah Mohammed put some imaginary snuff in his mouth, and said, "We captured five boys with long hair today. They were not wearing turbans. We shaved their heads and put them in prison. How long do you think we should keep them there?"

"Until their hair grows to their shoulders," Nabi replied matter-of-factly.

"What should we feed them with?" Faisal asked as he slapped his leg and scratched himself.

"You are my adviser," Nabi said, "You should tell me."

"We don't have enough food to eat ourselves," Faisal said. "Why not feed them with my lice? Or yours?" He picked something from Nabi's leg and offered it to him.

Nabi waved him off searched his pockets until he found some hashish. "When I smoke the holy bush, I can be calm. Then I will find a solution." He lit a cigarette, and rolled his eyes in a way that made him look as if he were quickly getting stoned. "We should feed them with one *naan* three times a day and some water. We have enough money in our budget for that, don't we, Finance Minister?"

Shah Mohammed spat out his imaginary snuff on the floor and searched his pockets for something. He found a small, wrinkled piece of paper. "Let me see our budget sheet," he said. He held the paper close to his eyes as if he were blind. "Why not only two *naan* a day per person? But they can have water as much as they need," he added generously. Then he corrected himself, "No, no, water only as much as is necessary for ablutions – three times a day, not five."

"Don't we have enough water for five times daily prayers?" Nabi asked.

"No," Shah Mohammed said shaking his head exaggeratedly. "With the drought, the water level in the prison wells is way down. After we pull out four hundred buckets, the water gets muddy and unusable."

"I have a better idea," Faisal said. "They must take their ablution only once a day in the morning and then keep themselves clean for the rest of the day."

"That means they cannot use the toilet for all the rest of the day," Shah Mohammed helpfully pointed out.

"Then they will not want to drink, and that will save more water," Faisal responded with delight.

Nabi slapped Faisal's back. "Brilliant!" he exclaimed. "That is why I keep you around as an adviser."

Faisal, in turn, slapped his leg. "Look. I killed a hundred lice," he said. Then he exploded with laughter. Nabi and Shah Mohammed did so as well. Some of the other actors standing around joined them, but some did not, because they had experienced Taliban prison. The memory was not funny.

Corinne did not understand a word of what had been said. When the interpreter tried to tell her, she held up her hand to him saying that she had understood as much as she needed from their performance, which left her laughing.

Corinne learned two things that day: the actors were very good comedians, and they knew how to work an audience.

If she did decide to go ahead with *Love's Labour's Lost*, she felt she would be comfortable casting Nabi Tanha, who had a powerful presence, Shah Mohammed, who projected dignity and power, and Faisal, who clearly had a natural gift for comic timing. And the older actor, Kabir Rahimi, who was again with them, had a smiling buoyancy that would be ideal for the pivotal role of the servant who carries messages between the men and the women and gets them all mixed up with hilarious results. But who could play the fourth noble?

∴∷∴

Over the next three days, many young men came to the Foundation to audition. They worked enthusiastically at doing improvisations, but Corinne could not see what she was looking for in any of them. Many of them confused acting with the overacting that they saw in the Bollywood movies that everyone in Afghanistan watched. She worked with each of them to see if she could help them tone down their performances, but with only limited success.

Then one afternoon Aref Bahunar showed up. Aref had that spark that every director looks for. A handsome young Hazara, he had a freshness about him. He understood subtlety and moved very well. His training at the university was evident. Corinne had him improvise a handful of scenes with some of the other actors and decided very quickly that she wanted him for the production.

"Are you making a movie?" he asked her. He was obviously disappointed when she told him, "No." Still, he was willing to stay and see what she could teach him.

With Aref on board, Corinne had four solid actors lined up for the young nobles, though she had not yet decided who would play which character. That meant that *Love's Labour's Lost* was halfway to being possible. It was time to gauge the actors' interest in it.

∴∷∴

With the four young men plus Kabir, Corinne met one afternoon to talk about Shakespeare's plays and to get their reactions to them. She started by explaining that Shakespeare had written tragedies and comedies, and they could think about doing any of them. The actors quickly made it clear that they wanted nothing to do with tragedy.

Nabi Tanha said, "We have lived tragedy for three decades of war. We want to do comedy."

Shah Mohammed agreed. "A tragedy play is too soon now. Let's make people laugh." He added, "When the time comes, we'll do a tragedy, and we will take our revenge. Revenge is like a thirst, but a thirst that cannot be quenched with water. The thirst of revenge can only be quenched by seeing the blood of enemies. We will show some blood on the stage to quench the great thirst of families of victims."

Corinne, who is notably articulate, was momentarily at a loss for words.

Aref then spoke very forcefully: "When we do a tragedy, we will write our own play, and not use Shakespeare's. Our tragedy will be far more intense than any tragedy he ever made. We will write it the way it happened: the planes came, circled high in the distance above us, then dropped bombs on our houses, our schools, our hospitals, and made them blast open as one collapsed after another, or sometimes several of them at the same time. Windows and doors blew out, and flames rose in giant mushroom-shaped smoke mixed with dust, and the air smelled of gunpowder, with women and children shouting out in fear or for help. The whole ground shook, and it felt like an earthquake. That is our tragedy, and we will write it. We will shake the stage and the audience to show what we went through. History can be recorded in books, but history shown on the stage is far more powerful."

Nabi had become fired up listening to Aref speak, and continued with his own narrative. "The Russians came and stayed ten years. When they withdrew," he said, "there then came the seven idiots from Pakistan." The actors all knew he meant: the seven factions who had been armed by the Americans to drive out the Russians, then subsequently turned their guns on one another. "And civil war started." Then he looked at Shah Mohammed, and shouted with blood lust, "I'm gonna kill you, because you're a Pashtun."

Shah Mohammed sprang to his feet as he rasped, "No, I'm gonna kill you, because you are a Hazara." They were improvising, but they had instantly sent a chill through the room. And then Faisal shouted, "I'm gonna kill you both, because neither of you is Uzbek," and everyone laughed. It was the first of many times that a well-timed joke by Faisal would defuse a situation that was heading towards becoming dangerously overheated.

Aref said, "And then came the black period, the Taliban, with their dirty *shalwar kameez*, their long black and white turbans, their mouths full of snuff, their eyes outlined by *kohl*, and ugly weapons hanging from their shoulders."

Nabi shouted in a coarse voice in Pashto, "School is banned for women. Nor are they allowed to work outside the house, and they should cover their heads when they go out."

Shah Mohammed, in an even harsher voice, continued, "All men should grow beards and be present in the mosque five times a day for prayers."

"No one can keep pigeons or any fighting birds or animals in the house," Faisal added in a deep Kandahari-accented Pashto. "We will monitor everything, and if we find anyone with fighting birds or animals, we will punish them." He looked at everyone like a Taliban, with fierce eyes, until he suddenly exploded in laughter. And they all laughed. Then, he made fierce eyes again, and they all stopped laughing. He continued, "No kite flying for kids or anyone else." Again, he burst out laughing, and everyone else did, too. He was revealing a power as an actor that he had not displayed previously.

Every actor had a story to tell as they recounted the history of the past three decades in Afghanistan, from the invasion of the Russians in 1979 to the arrival of the Americans in 2001. Corinne listened to them thoughtfully, and asked many questions. As she did, the actors realized that there were large gaps in her knowledge of Afghanistan's history, cultures and customs. They saw that their time with her would be a two-way conversation. She would teach them about theater and Shakespeare; they would teach her about Afghanistan.

Settling In

Kabul. April 2005.

Corinne was beginning to feel at home in Kabul. Her days were focused on the play. Her evenings centered on quiet meals with her friend David, for which he proudly sourced nearly everything from Afghanistan. His risotto used rice from Kunduz that he infused with saffron from Helmand. His mushrooms came from the Panjshir valley, his fresh cumin from Badakhshan, his olive oil from Jalalabad, and his yogurt from a woman who owned a cow and lived in another part of the old fort. Somehow he always managed to have a couple of bottles of good wine on hand as well.

The interpreter had arranged a driver for Corinne. His name was Daoud. He did not speak much English, but every day, as she was coping with heat, dust and an impossibly long list of things to accomplish, he would buoyantly shuttle her around Kabul, using many alleys and lanes that not even the donkey drivers knew. Hours later, when she was exhausted, and sometimes discouraged after a disappointing rehearsal, he whisked her from the Foundation to the old fort faster than any armored convoy, all the while generating a soothing presence that would take the edge off anybody's anxieties by telling one joke after another. The interpreter was sometimes laughing too hard to translate. It did not hurt that Daoud had movie star good looks and a radiant smile.

:::::

Slowly Corinne was getting to know more about the five actors she had cast. One day Corinne asked each of the *bacha ha*, "the boys," as she was now calling them, why he had become interested in acting.

Faisal smiled, and said, "Acting is an art, like painting, wood carving or calligraphy. None of these arts are easy when you first start, but once you are in the sea of it, you'll go on swimming for the rest of your life, even though you know that you can never really reach your destination. I became addicted to acting at school when everybody clapped for me after I performed the role of a lazy student on Teacher's Day. I was ten or twelve years old. I was immediately addicted to it, as some people are to opium, or a bee is to flower nectar. But I didn't learn it in an academic way. I've never been to an acting class in my life. When you have the hunger for something, and you don't have a school, your talent becomes your school."

Nabi, by contrast, told Corinne how he had studied acting at Kabul University's Faculty of Fine Arts. "I'm not just an actor," he said. "I also write screenplays, I direct movies, I montage and edit movies. I act in both movies and theater, and I'm a good camera-man, too." Looking straight at her, he suggested, "You should watch my television series *Bulbul*, which is very famous. And I'm very popular, too. When I go out, people call me Bulbul, as if my real name is Bulbul."

Whenever Shah Mohammed was about to speak, he rocked forward and back a couple of times, the way some people clear their throat. When Nabi had finished speaking, Shah Moham-med rocked forward twice. "Everything I know about acting," he said, "I learned from my good friend and teacher, Nabi Tanha. I didn't learn acting in an academic way. I learned it from Nabi jan, by doing it."

When Nabi directed a movie, Shah Mohammed was his assis-tant. When Nabi wrote a screenplay, Shah Mohammed was his assistant. When Nabi was a cameraman for a movie, Shah Moham-med was his assistant. Nabi and Shah Mohammed got into loud arguments all the time, but five minutes later they laughed at whatever had come between them. Shah Mohammed had worked for eighteen years in Afghanistan television as an editor, cameraman, and archivist. Now, with Nabi, he was making commercials for Afghanistan's fast-growing number of television networks.

"After the Taliban collapsed," Shah Mohammed went on, "I stepped into the world of movies and discovered what it means to be an actor."

Kabir Rahimi was the oldest among the actors. He always sat in a corner and, although he was always ready with a smile, he did not say much. Once he mentioned that he too had studied acting at Kabul University. "I directed a few movies and plays, and I'm a playwright for both movies and the theater," he told them. "I can easily get the picture of a situation, and put it into a play, and make it funny."

Afghans rarely talk about their personal or family lives to strangers. When Corinne asked them questions about themselves, the actors were polite, but vague. Over time, though, as she and the actors began to get to know one another, the individuals behind the actors' masks came more clearly into focus.

Nabi was married with several children, including twins. He had the north Asian features of his Mongolian ancestors, whose descendants had come to Afghanistan in numerous waves as Turkmen, Hazara, Uzbek, Qizilbash and others. Some look almost Chinese; others appear quite different owing to extensive intermarriage over the centuries. Afghans are ethnically very mixed, but usually identify only with their fathers' people. About his own father, Nabi would say only that he was a farmer.

Shah Mohammed was a Tajik. He and his wife were the only ones of all their relatives who lived in Afghanistan. All the rest were in Europe, Canada or America. Shah Mohammed had had several chances to leave, but turned them all down. "Perhaps I am mad," he said, "but I love Afghanistan."

His wife was a teacher at a school for girls. They had six children and wanted them to live in an Islamic society, especially their five daughters. He did not want them to grow up with the values of the young people he saw in the Western media. All his children were getting good educations. His goal, he said, was for each of his daughters to obtain a university degree before he gave permission for her to marry.

Aref had grown up in a poor family. No one in his family had ever been an actor. He had a wife who, like himself, was a Hazara. She lived with his parents in Ghazni province, about two hours south of Kabul on the road to Kandahar. Their marriage had been arranged by their fathers. They had no children. One afternoon he boasted playfully that, "In a few years there will be a team of football players in my house, and I'll be the trainer." As a student at Kabul University, he had very few chances to visit his family. He could go home, he said, only about once a month for a day or two.

::::::

When Corinne asked the actors to talk about their lives during the war years, they grew quiet.

Shah Mohammed said, "Why should I give you a headache with my sad stories? Our history in my lifetime is nothing but war. Why should I bore you with that?"

Nabi bewailed, "People are so stupid fighting for a king or a president whom they never will see. There would have been fewer wars if the leaders had to fight each other, rather than sending young men onto bloodthirsty battlefields."

Faisal added, "The men who are the most powerful are the most foolish, while lesser men are really wiser and good men."

"Like me?" Nabi said.

"Like all of us," Kabir said with a sad smile.

Aref had been quiet during this conversation. He sighed deeply, saying: "I'm a man of sense, or at least try to be. I don't let myself be disturbed by the ups and downs of life. I learned this from my father. I may be rich or poor, but neither matters to me. What is important to me is always having respect for other human beings and trying not to injure them or their feelings. I always try my best to forgive them if they injure me. My conscience is more important to me than my anger for revenge at those who injured me physically or psychologically during those years of war. I have no fear of death, for it is a natural thing, even if it doesn't always happen naturally."

Everyone was quiet for a few moments. Then Faisal started telling a story that he would tell many times again. Whenever he told it, he always had a radiant smile, as if he were being reminded of an old joke that was still very funny to him.

One day a couple of years before, he said, he was hanging out with five of his closest friends in front of their houses, not far from the front door of the Foundation. All of them had grown up in that neighborhood and had known each other since they were little kids flying homemade kites from the rooftops. Without warning, a rocket hit the ground a few steps from where they were standing. It exploded, and all five of his friends were killed instantly.

"I'm the only one who survived," he said, his eyes strangely gleeful. Then he showed them the mass of scars on his thighs, arm and back. "This is my gift from Hekmatyar," he chortled, referring to the notoriously brutal leader of one of the factions, Gulbuddin Hekmatyar.

At the end Faisal would always say, "By now I should have been turned into dust by the worms in my grave, but God saved me, and here I am doing Shakespeare." Then he would laugh. "This Shakespeare fellow should be proud of me, right?"

Casting the Girls

Kabul. March 2005.

Every morning before she went to the police station, Breshna Bahar sat at her dressing table putting on multiple layers of eye shadow and painting her lips red. She did not look like a grandmother. She seemed, rather, to be in her late thirties. Her neighbors thought that she was single and that her two daughters were her younger sisters. Only a small number knew that she was a widow.

Breshna was one of the few women in Kabul who drove a car. She had started driving only days after the Taliban had been routed from Kabul four years earlier. A few months later, she got back her old job as a detective with the Kabul police department.

Though she was not a tall woman, when she sat in the driver's seat of her gray Toyota Corolla wearing her green police uniform and large black sunglasses, she looked like she owned the whole country. Anyone who saw her immediately recognized her as the television character Gul Chera, but no one dared to call her by that name when she was in uniform. She studiously wore a frown whenever she was in public.

When she arrived at the police station, she greeted her colleagues in the reception area and headed to her office. The interior of the building was painted a dingy shade of yellow. Every room had a few tables and chairs along with bookshelves where files were stacked. Only the chief had a computer on his desk. A thick layer of dust covered the computer; it looked as if it had never been used.

That morning, before Breshna had a chance to pour herself a glass of tea, one of the other officers pushed a criminal into her office. "Here's your work for today." A man in a *shalwar kameez* stood in front of her in handcuffs. The officer sat on the chair next to Breshna's table while the criminal remained standing sullenly.

"What did he do?" Breshna asked quietly.

The officer put two bags of opium on Breshna's table. "We found this in his car. It's parked in the courtyard. Go look for yourself," he said.

"Put him in the cell," Breshna said as she rose and headed outside with her camera and notebook.

Breshna ordered a heavy-set officer to bring dogs to sniff a red Toyota Corolla parked in the courtyard on the side of the police station. While she waited, she lit a cigarette, inhaling deeply as she examined the car. She found two more bags of opium under the seats, one in the trunk, and another hidden under the engine. She took photos of everything.

The gate to the street swung open and a black Land Cruiser drove in. The chief of her station climbed out of the back seat. He was a tall man, and his uniform was neatly pressed. "Salaam, Breshna," he said.

"Salaam, sir," Breshna said.

"What have you got?"

"I found these," Breshna pointed to the bags of drugs.

"Is he the man you've been looking for?" the chief asked.

"He could be. If not, he'll lead me to him. I'll know more after I interrogate him."

As the chief was leaving, Breshna heard a commotion in the reception area. She went back inside and found Nabi, dressed in a white shirt and jeans. All her colleagues, including the chief, wanted have their photos taken with him. Nabi posed and smiled as the cameras flashed.

"What brought you here?" Breshna snorted when everyone had gone to their offices.

"A woman has come from France and is directing a play. By

Shakespeare," he said. "She wants to meet some actresses. Come to the Foundation when you're done with your work here and you can find out the details."

"I have a lot to do today."

"You must, woman!" Nabi tried to sound like his character from *Bulbul*.

"You may be my husband in *Bulbul*, but not in real life," Breshna replied in a coarse voice edged with laughter. "Always remember that."

"Thanks for reminding me. Sometimes it is hard to know what is real and what is not. I can't tell the difference anymore. Everywhere I go, people call me Bulbul and ask about my wife Gul Chera. And here you are, and you don't act like Gul Chera."

"Stop being silly, Nabi, or I'll put you next to that man in the cell."

"All right, officer!" Nabi saluted Breshna, then turned around and left.

::::::

On the day of the first audition for actresses, an unseasonably early heat wave was sweeping over Kabul, chasing away the mountain air that is usually still cool in May. When Corinne arrived at the Foundation with the interpreter, a group of women were already sitting on chairs arranged in small groups on the grassy lawn, chatting with one another. Some were young, some middle-aged, some old. When they saw Corinne and her interpreter come into the garden, they stood up as a sign of respect to greet them.

Corinne introduced herself and described the production she was planning. She told them that she needed five good talented actresses. It soon became evident, however, that many of the women had never appeared on stage or in front of a camera. Several were housewives who just wanted to do something different. With the Taliban gone, they had thrown open the cage of the *burqa*, and were ready to fly. They had decided to become actresses, to express their hopes and sorrows through acting.

When Corinne asked them to do an improvisation as an audition, they all looked puzzled. None knew what an improvisation was, except for a tall girl named Leila who had come with her mother.

Corinne asked her how she knew about improvisations.

"My father is an actor," she replied. "He is often on television. Maybe you have seen him?"

Corinne shook her head as she asked, "What would you like to do?"

"I will be an angry mother who is buried under too much housework."

"Go ahead," Corinne told her.

Leila stood up, rolled up her sleeves, and pretended that she was slicing onions. As she wiped tears from her eyes with the back of her hand, she shouted at her kids to get out of the kitchen. Then one of them knocked all her spices onto the kitchen floor. As she gathered them up, a pot she had on the stove caught fire. The kids started crying as her husband came in and shouted at her. She yelled back at him to help her pour water on the fire, but instead he came and beat her with a ladle, a pot and a plate. All the time the children kept crying, and everything was a complete mess.

Leila finished. Corinne clapped, and everyone else did as well. Corinne looked at Leila's mother and said, "Your daughter is very good, especially for a girl who has never acted before." Leila's mother's smiled appreciatively when the interpreter told her what Corinne had said. Jokingly, Corinne asked, "Was she pretending to be you?"

Leila's mother's face turned red. "No," she said abruptly. After a few seconds, though, she smiled again and said, "Maybe."

Corinne asked Leila about herself. Leila told her that, though she was eighteen, she was in the seventh grade. Like many young Afghans, she had had few opportunities for formal schooling during the war years, because either they were living in refugee camps where schools did not exist, or they had remained in the Taliban's Afghanistan, where girls were forbidden to study. Leila and her family had fled to Iran. She spoke Dari with a strong Farsi accent. A couple of times the interpreter had to ask her to repeat what she had said.

Now all the other women understood what improvisation meant. They wanted to do their own. They started moving their chairs back to create a space in which to perform. Among them was Breshna Bahar. As she stood up to begin, several of the other women recognized her and nodded to one another.

Just the way Breshna stood showed that she was accustomed to being in charge. She started to explain what she wanted to do, but Corinne stopped her and told her instead to show it in her acting.

"All right," she said in English. She lay down on the floor with one elbow resting on a pillow, fingering an imaginary beard. Everyone quickly understood that she was impersonating a man.

In a deep, rough voice, the man for called his daughter. He demanded a glass of green tea, and when she gave it to him, he took one sip and spat it out. He looked at his imaginary daughter and shouted angrily, "Is this tea, or donkey's piss? Why is it cold? Why is the cardamom missing? You are behaving like your bitch mother. Do you know why I killed her? Because she was disrespectful! Get me some good tea, you daughter of a whore!"

There was some soft murmuring among the women watching at the coarse language that Breshna was using. But they were also nodding in recognition.

Then the man turned his head away, but kept shouting after the daughter. "When you have done that, tidy the house. There are some suitors coming today. One of them is the Khan of the upper town. He is asking for your hand. I said 'Yes' to him in the field yesterday. He is coming with his family to make it official."

Then the man looked up at the daughter, and asked harshly, "Why are you crying? Say again? You are too young to be married? Who says so? I know you learned these things from your whore mother."

The man changed his tone to what he probably thought was reasonable. "You are sixteen. Sixteen is marriageable. What did you say? Speak louder! The Khan is older than you? So what? He is my age. Are you telling me that I'm too old, and I can't marry a sixteen year old? You can't find better than the Khan. He is the leader of his tribe. What did you say? He has two more wives? So what? He is allowed to marry four wives. Who are you to say what you will do? I'm your father, and I will decide. Stop crying, or I'll crush you under my feet." The man continued fingering his imaginary beard.

Suddenly, the man became the actress again, and Breshna burst out laughing. She looked at Corinne, and asked in English, "Good?"

"Very good!" Corinne said, "And look, you speak English."

"A little," she said with a hint of shyness that had not been evident in her improvisation.

"You are a good actor," Corinne said.

"Thank you," she said in English.

"What is your name?"

"Breshna Bahar," she said.

"Where did you learn acting?" Corinne asked.

She did not understand the question, so the interpreter repeated it in Dari.

"I've been acting for several years. I'm known for my part in the *Bulbul* series with Nabi Tanha. I'm Gul Chera. When people on the street see me, that is what they call me."

"Okay, Breshna jan. I'll talk to you later," Corinne told her. Corinne had already picked up the Afghan habit of adding "jan" to someone's name. It is a sign of affection and respect. And Afghans say it to almost everyone, whether or not they actually have any affection or respect for them.

:::::

The next day, a new group of women were waiting at the Foundation, more than ten in all. They were all asked to do improvisations. None were as good as Breshna or Leila, but they left their phone numbers before saying their goodbyes.

Corinne was about to leave the Foundation for home when Parwin Mushtahel arrived. She apologized for being late, explaining that she had been stuck in one of Kabul's terrible traffic jams that clog the streets several times a day.

Corinne explained that she was about to leave and would prefer to see her the next day, but Parwin insisted, explaining that it was difficult for her to come the great distance from her home to the Foundation. She wanted to do the audition and be done with it. In the end, Corinne agreed and led the way into the grand salon where it was quieter.

Parwin announced, "I'd like to do an improvisation about a widowed woman who lost her husband and son in the civil war, and now she is going to commit suicide. But before she hangs herself, she wants the world to know what she went through, and why she is ending her life."

Corinne looked hesitant, and said, "I think that's a little too grim."

"It is based on real life," Parwin said, "In fact, the woman was our neighbor."

"OK, let's do it," Corinne said. Feeling a little tired because of the hot weather, she sat down on one of the long, flat *toshaks* on the floor, and leaned against a wall.

Parwin carried a chair to the middle of the room, then climbed onto it. Her face turned serious, and she began. "Life has no meaning for me anymore. Life lost its meaning on the day that a rocket from Gulbuddin landed on our roof, and took my son away from me forever. He was only eight years old, but so handsome. Large dark brown eyes, a little nose, curly black hair, smooth and spotless skin.

"I bathed him, played with him, splashed water on him, played hide and seek with him, made sand palaces with him, drew animals with him, and flew kites with him. He couldn't pronounce the letter 'S.' Only 'Sh.'

"My Omar used to tell me strange and funny stories, all the work of his imagination. He used to start this way: 'There was a jungle that had many animals. They were all friends with each other. They had kings. All the kings had wings. God made them kings from their birth.'

"I asked him, 'What about snakes or elephants?'

"He said, 'Their kings had wings, too.'

"I asked him, 'What about the birds? They all have wings already. Were they all kings?'

"He thought for a second and said, 'There are no birds in that forest.'"

Parwin was making Omar feel present in the room. She went on.

"Life in those days was nothing but a chain of struggles, of fear and of death. But you, Omar jan, made my black days as bright as the sun. And one day while I was in the kitchen cooking for you, your favourite dessert, *ferni* [rice custard], a blind rocket from Gulbuddin landed on your room where you were still asleep, and you still had not told me your dreams from that night. During the years of civil war, thousands of rockets were blind. They didn't land where they were supposed to land, but on people's houses. We called those rockets blind.

"The noise of the rocket was so loud that I could not hear anything. I was dizzy, and everything smelled of gunpowder, and dust was everywhere as if it had conquered the whole earth. I staggered to your room, and saw a big mound of rubble, all in a pile, the roof beams, the mud bricks. But there was no trace of you. Several times I yelled, 'Omar jan, where are you?', but I didn't hear your sweet voice. I continued shouting.

"My shouts were echoing inside my own skull, a hundred times louder than ever before. I yelled so much that I lost my voice. I noticed the neighbors had come into the courtyard, all the men standing around me, watching me, but none of them dared to come close to me. I was like a madwoman, slapping myself, crying, pulling my hair and tearing my clothes, but no one calmed me.

"Your father Karim came home. He had only just gone out to get some fresh bread for breakfast. When he saw me in such a state, he covered me with his *patu*, but I kept sobbing. He took me in his arms, and kissed me on my head as he said again and again, 'Calm down, calm down.' But how could I calm down? I had just lost my sweetheart, my Omar. I had lost my calmness forever. I won't ever feel like a human again. I was something else now. I continued crying as I lost consciousness."

As Parwin stood on the chair, she was creating a whole universe centered on this woman's pain and despair. Corinne's interpreter did his best to keep up with what Parwin was saying and whisper it into Corinne's ear.

"When I woke up, I found myself in my bed alone, and the sun was pouring into the room. I didn't know why I was sleeping at such an hour of the day. It was almost midday. I had a terrible headache. I went to the mirror to tidy myself before going out, but I saw something in the mirror that scared me to my core. It was the face of a woman with disheveled hair, a scratched face, eyes red like fireballs, and torn clothes. 'Who is this woman?' I asked myself. 'Is this me? What happened to me?'

"Suddenly, the mirror shattered into bits, and I could no longer see myself. I ran out of the room to find out what had happened. All I could see was a cloud of dust rising to the sky. I knew right away that another of Gulbuddin's blind rockets had landed on the same room where you, my son, had been buried under all that rubble. And this time, this rocket had killed your father who had been trying to dig your body from under the pile of dirt.

"My eyes were dry. There was not a single tear left to come out. So instead, I laughed. I laughed: 'Ha ha ha ha ha ha ha ...' Soon all the neighbors came again, and saw me laughing. This time, their women came too. They thought I had lost my mind, but they didn't know I was crying with my laughter. I noticed the women weeping for me, and I felt jealous towards them that they had tears to shed for me, yet I had no tears to shed for my husband and my sweetheart little boy. I laughed, 'Ha ha ha ha ha ha ...'"

Parwin filled the room with a chilling laugh that sent shivers down Corinne's spine. Her eyes grew wide now as she picked up something in front of her.

"I found a piece of metal. It was a fragment of the blind rocket. It was sharp like a butcher's knife. I lifted it up to stab into my stomach, but I was grabbed by a man who gripped my wrists. I struggled, but couldn't succeed. I lost consciousness again, and collapsed. When I woke up, I saw my sister looking at me. She kissed me, and told me that I had been sleeping for four days. 'Why for so long?' I asked myself. Suddenly, I remembered everything. I cried. This time, really crying. Not laughing. I didn't just cry for my husband and son, I cried for not having been there to cry on the day when their coffins had been taken out of the house. I cried for what I saw. I cried for my future. I cried that I will never be able to smile again. I cried for all those mothers and widows who have lost their dear ones. I cried for my country. I cried for everything that is wrong in our lives."

Tears were streaming down Parwin's cheeks.

"My eyes were like springs, and tears continued falling, wetting my face, burning my cheeks. Everything looked blurry, and tears still kept coming. From that day, I never stopped. I know that my heart will keep crying until the moment of death. I don't know when death will claim me. Maybe not for a very long time. So today I'm going to claim death. I want to stop this crying in my heart. My dear ones are in paradise. I want to see them. And today I shall. The journey is short. This rope in my hands is my transportation."

Parwin held up an imaginary rope and a frightening kind of joy filled her face.

"One end of this rope is tied to the ceiling. This end is in my hands. I will put it around my neck, and then I will push the chair from under my feet. I know it is going to be painful. But pain has no meaning for me anymore. Physical pain is nothing compared with the pain in my heart and my soul.

"Let me take a last good look at this room. The floor is covered with carpets that Karim and I bought. I remember buying that TV with him, and that videocassette player. The first tape we watched was of our wedding. I remember that green cradle in the corner of the room. Omar jan grew up in it. He would have been fifteen years old by now, as handsome as his father. Seven years have passed without him. Seven years! All these years, I cried even in my dreams. Now it is time for laughing. I have to go, and laugh with my Omar jan and my Karim jan. We will laugh together. Oh my God! I'm smiling now. After seven years, I'm smiling. A smile is a promise of laughter. Goodbye, cries. Laughter, wait for me. I'm coming towards you. I'm very close. Here, I'm coming." Then she pushed the chair from under her feet.

Corinne's eyes had welled up with tears. The tragic energy Parwin had generated transcended language barriers. While Corinne fought back tears, Parwin stood in front of her and the interpreter with a warm smile on her face.

Corinne clapped. The interpreter covered his eyes and quietly wept. For years, he had not cried and knew that he must be brave, swallow his sorrows, shut his eyes against his tears and keep them there. He knew that he could not defeat them once they took control of him.

Suddenly, Parwin started to cry, as if all the interpreter's tears had found a new home in her eyes. Corinne rose quickly and hugged her and started rubbing her back, but she sobbed as she shook in Corinne's arms.

The interpreter had to walk away and make a slow turn around the garden. Later he told Corinne, "I couldn't stand being there for another minute. How many nights had we sat in the basement of our house as bombs fell around us? How many days had we known that this was our last day on earth? How many screams had we heard when our neighbors had been hit by rockets, or had been knocked deaf by the blast that killed all sound when it exploded too close?"

He explained to Corinne on the ride home to the old fort that, "Parwin was narrating my childhood. From the time I turned ten, the Mujahedin started fighting their cruel and pointless war. Not even the Russians, whom we had hated and defeated, treated us as badly as the factional commanders of the Mujahedin. For four years, day after day, year after year, I lived through what Parwin described."

He sat at the far end of the garden for several minutes until he could push all these unwanted memories back into the deep hole of the past where he had tried so hard to keep them. By the time he returned to the audition room, Parwin was calm, though her eyes were still glistening. She apologized to the interpreter for stirring up his emotions. The interpreter simply said, *"Mushkel n'ast,"* Dari for "No problem".

Corinne asked the interpreter if he were OK. He smiled, "Yes," though it was clear that he was still sobbing in his heart of hearts for that woman, whom only God knows if she was still alive or was with her husband and her son.

As Corinne watched him grapple with his feelings, she understood with the utmost clarity how deeply Afghans were in mourning for themselves, their loved ones and the country that had been taken from them. She saw how emotions borne of war memories were never far from the surface. If she had not fully understood before why the actors had not wanted to do a tragedy, she did now.

Her voice was unusually warm when she spoke. "Parwin jan, you are a good actress. Though our play is not about tragedy, you are very gifted, and I'd like you to be part of it."

A shy smile appeared on Parwin's face as the interpreter translated. Parwin hugged Corinne again.

"Was she a close friend?" Corinne asked. "Your neighbor?"

Parwin shrugged. "We knew each other," she said. "Her brother and sisters moved away a few weeks later. I never saw any of them again. That is how it is here in Afghanistan. We never know how things end." A few minutes later, she left.

::::::

No one liked good conversation more than Corinne, and if it led to a strongly argued philosophical debate, all the better. That evening, though, she was unusually pensive. She hardly touched the glass of merlot that David had poured for her as she told him about Parwin's audition.

"Everybody in Kabul must have stories like that," she said quietly.

"Everybody in Afghanistan," he added as he swirled a soup he was making on the stove.

"Has anyone considered setting up a Truth and Reconciliation Commission the way they did in South Africa?"

"It gets mentioned," he said. "But where is the Mandela to give it moral force?"

She sipped her wine and told him he was putting too much salt in the soup. Their conversation went off in other directions. For the rest of the evening, though, she kept thinking about the woman whose tragedy Parwin had so movingly portrayed.

:::::

The next day, none of the women who came to audition had had any previous experience. They tried hard, but were not ready to perform. Among them was a woman who looked to be about eighty years old. She was barely four feet tall. Corinne politely told her, "I don't have a part for you in this play. Maybe the next one." She kept the woman's phone number anyway, because she was getting worried that she might not find anyone else.

A day later, a tall woman with a lot of makeup was among those who came to audition. Her eyelashes were covered in heavy mascara, and her eyebrows had high arches blackened by eyebrow pencil. She was Saba Sahar.

The interpreter spoke to her with the enthusiasm of a fan, gushing, "It is a great pleasure meeting you! I've seen several of your movies, and I liked them all."

"Thank you very much!" Saba said graciously, smiling.

The interpreter had not expected to see Saba at the auditions, assuming that she would not work for the low wages being offered. As if reading his mind, Saba said, "I've heard some interesting things about Corinne, and I was told by the Foundation that she is going to do Shakespeare. I love Shakespeare. It is not something that we often have had a chance to do. I'd like to be a part of it."

Corinne asked Saba if she could do some improvisations. Saba gave a look that suggested that she felt she was too well established in her profession to be asked to improvise.

Not knowing Saba's background, Corinne turned to the interpreter with a look that asked, "What is it with her? Does she think she is too good for us?" He shrugged, not wanting to get caught between two strong personalities.

Saba asked whom she was supposed to play. Corinne replied, "Anything that you're comfortable with." Then she changed her mind, suggesting, "Why not play a policewoman, since you have done that in many of your movies?"

"Since this is for Shakespeare, I would rather do something royal, if you don't mind," Saba responded.

"Go ahead," Corinne said.

"I'm going to play a Persian princess whose fiancé is from Iraq," she said as she looked around at everyone in the room. "He has left her for another woman, whom everyone thinks of as a prostitute. It's like a Shakespeare play. Shakespeare is all about love, betrayals, lies, killings, disappearances, mysteries, sadism, absurdisms, because these topics don't get old. After all, all our lives encompass these things."

"You seem to know quite a lot about Shakespeare," Corinne interrupted.

"He is one of my favorite playwrights," Saba said as she walked to the center of the room. "I used to do Shakespeare at the university. I enjoy his irony, his unpredictability, yet his writing is so clear and poetic." When she turned to face them again, she had become a different person as she launched into her improvisation with a cold whisper.

"I don't understand him. Why did he betray me? Every angle I consider turns into a puzzle for me. How, after so much love and patience, after so many declarations, vows, sighs, tears, obsessions, passionate letters, ardent protestations, and repeated promises could he have betrayed me – not just me, but my family, my country, his family and his country? What does that whore have that I don't? What happened to all those promises?"

She had immediately snared Corinne's attention. Most of the other women who had auditioned previously had rooted themselves in one place. Saba, however, was moving all over the room, as if she were in a house where she had lived all her life. She made everyone else there feel like intruders.

"I was not in love with him, and I still am not. But I was falling in love with him. I had dreamed that by marrying him I would bury myself in passion forever. He used to tell me I was gorgeous. He used to whisper into my ears, 'Your beauty delights me whenever I look at you.' He told me, 'I want to give over to the sweet violence of love, and let you rule me. I had thousands of hearts offered to me, but when I saw you, I gave them all up. Now I love only you, and have you alone in my heart.' Was he lying? Why? But now I know why. Men are liars? No, not all men. Not Rumi. He was in love all his life, though his love was for God, while mine was for God's creation. Maybe love is not true unless it is for God. No! Love is madness. Love is stupidity. Love is betrayal. Or maybe love is only a mere and empty word, and we give it all kinds of meanings.

"I believe in God, but I don't believe in love now. I don't believe in many things now. Man is one of them. No! Many men are decent. Our prophets were men. They told us of truth. They led us to the right path, the one that leads to God. Men are not all bad. Only this one."

Saba's voice was now low and cool, filled with the fire of scorn.

"Ah, a breaker is always a breaker. He broke my heart, and he will break hers, whoever he is with now. The fault is not his, but mine. I was fooled by his sweet words, while I should have studied his manners and learned his real motives. He didn't fool me, but himself. I'm not the real victim, but he is. His betrayals towards so many will turn people against him. He is not making friends, but fierce foes, and they will bring about his end one day. As for me, I must restore my belief in men. I need time for that. Time and patience; they are key to unlocking the miseries and opening the doors to happiness. Time and patience."

She stopped, and remained motionless for several moments. Everyone watching did as well. The interpreter had had difficulty translating what Saba said because she had used a high form of Dari that is usually found only in literature. She was speaking almost like poetry. The best he could do had been to provide the gist of it for Corinne while somehow capturing the excitement of hearing her throw poetic couplets into the air like rose petals.

Corinne seemed to have understood this. Language does not have to be a barrier between theater artists. They can comprehend each other in other ways.

"I very much enjoyed what you did," Corinne said to Saba.

Saba acknowledged the compliment with a slight nod. Corinne told Saba that she would like to have her in the cast. Saba asked Corinne to let her know a week in advance of the start of rehearsals, because she had many projects of her own. In the Afghan way, she asked permission to leave, then walked gracefully out of the room.

:::::

All the other women who had come to audition that day felt small with Saba Sahar there. They all knew they could not perform as well as she had done. Two of them quietly walked out of the room soon after she did and never came back.

The auditioning continued for a couple of more days, and many more women came, but none had the skills needed. Corinne took their phone numbers and told them that the interpreter would call to let them know whether they had been selected for the play. They thanked her and left.

:::::

Marina Golbahari was probably the best known actress in Afghanistan. Now, with the pressure on to find one more experienced woman for the play, Corinne was anxious to locate her. Marina had broken hearts around the world two years earlier when she had played the title role in the film *Osama*. But where was she? Corinne asked Robert if he could help find her. He said he would try, but even he did not know where to look.

Searching for Marina

Kabul. June 2005

When the film *Osama* had been released in 2003, the news media in Kabul were filled with stories about Marina Golbahari. *Osama* was Afghanistan's first entry in the Cannes Film Festival, and Marina was celebrated as the face of Afghanistan's newly emerging film industry.

Marina played the role of a young girl who pretends to be a boy during the madness of the Taliban, so she can earn money for her impoverished family. Filmgoers could not take their eyes off her. Her face was like an encyclopedia of human emotions, as one after another swept across it.

Her own story was as touching. Her family had sunk into desperate poverty during the years of civil war. She was forced to beg in the streets in Kabul. She would go to restaurants and ask to have scraps from the tables. On a good day, she would get a few kebab leftovers wrapped in *naan*, or maybe even a few crumpled notes from someone who felt compassion.

One day she had gone to beg for food from the restaurant table where film director Siddiq Barmak was eating. At the time, he was looking for a young girl to cast as Osama. He was struck by Marina's charisma. She had a certain something that he had not seen in any of the girls he had auditioned.

He did a few shots of her with a small video camera he had with him, and was amazed at the way her personality filled the screen.

He asked her to take him to meet her father. She was about ten years old at the time, though like many Afghans was not entirely sure of her age.

Within months, Marina would go from begging to being a cinema celebrity. Fame in Afghanistan, however, does not come with a fixed address. No one at the Foundation nor among the actors whom Corinne had met knew where Marina lived. Siddiq Barmak would surely have known, but he was out of the country and could not be reached.

Some said that she still lived in a refugee camp near Kabul Stadium. One morning, Corinne went there with the interpreter. The camp had been a small city of tents for many years. When they arrived, however, they found that only a few tents were still in place. The United Nations, which had been running the camp, was in the process of shutting it down that week. Its residents were being moved into permanent shelter. Marina's family was not there, and none of the few refugees remaining knew where she lived; in fact, they had never heard of her. However, a few weeks later, Barmak returned to Kabul, and Robert learned from him that Marina's family had settled in a poor neighborhood known as Char Qala-e-Wazir Abad.

∴∴∴

Marina's house was on a small backstreet, with a narrow drainage ditch running down the middle filled with the human waste from the toilets of the houses on both sides. Kabul has no sewers, despite all the aid that foreign governments claim to have given. Thousands of flies that had been dancing in the ditch flew up in large swarms into the faces of Corinne and the interpreter, displeased at having been disturbed. Their buzzing was loud enough to be frightening. The stink from the ditch was overwhelming.

The interpreter knocked on a metal gate that he guessed was Marina's. Inside, dogs started barking. A minute later, a little girl opened the door a crack. The interpreter told her that Corinne and he were there to see her sister, Marina.

The girl shouted, "Marina, Marina, Marina, here are some people who want to see you." Corinne, holding her head scarf in front of her nose, noted with relief, "The right house." The little girl looked up at Corinne and the interpreter and smiled.

Marina ran towards the gate, barefoot. Before she even said hello, she giggled. She opened the door wide for the visitors to walk in. Then she said, "Salaam, please come in. *Kaka* [uncle] Barmak told me about you."

Inside the small courtyard, two massive dogs chained to a stake in the ground were barking nonstop. Next to a well were some unwashed dishes. Marina said that she had been washing them until she had heard an Indian song on TV that she liked, and had left them for later. She led the way to a small room with *toshak* cushions arranged along the walls. A TV in the corner was still showing the Indian song. A Bollywood actress named Kajol was singing and dancing with actor Shah Rukh Khan.

"I tried to find you at the refugee camp near the stadium," Corinne said.

Marina giggled again. "We moved from there a long time ago," she said. "My film career enabled me to buy this small house."

Corinne started telling her a little about the project.

"I would love to work with you," Marina said. "I'll learn a lot of new things about acting. But I've never done theater before. What is theater exactly? I have heard the word, but don't know what it means."

When Corinne tried to explain, Marina giggled.

"Is it without cutting and stopping?" she asked.

"Yes, there are no cameras," Corinne said. "You have to be on stage for two hours, and cannot miss a word."

Marina widened her eyes. "Oh, that is not possible!" she said.

"Yes it is," Corinne said. "People have been doing it for centuries. Are you still going to school?" Corinne asked.

"I was in the fourth grade," Marina replied. She said that she had been discouraged from going to school by some people whose names she did not want to reveal. "They tell me that I don't need to because I'm a famous actress now." The headmaster at her school had told her, "You have to decide, either your studies or the movies." So she had stopped going to school.

The dogs outside barked a few times. Marina got up to see if anyone had come, but the dogs were looking at the sky.

"Silly creatures," Marina said. "They are barking at the kites." Then she giggled. "I'm being impolite talking to you here, I should go and get you some tea." She left. A few minutes later, she returned with a tray. She served green tea in a blue Chinese pot with cups on their saucers arranged on an ornate silver tray. As she poured tea in the cups, the smell of cardamom arose. She said that for her role in *Osama*, she was paid $6,000. Some of that money had been used to buy beautiful things for her family's new house.

Corinne asked her question after question about her family, the other films she had made since *Osama*, Siddiq Barmak and life in Afghanistan. Marina giggled more than she talked. "I'm one of ten brothers and sisters," she said. "All from one mother. Two of my sisters are married and live separately with their husbands. One in Iran and another in Kabul. I lost two older sisters in the civil war. The rest are living in this little courtyard."

Her father used to sell Bollywood audio cassettes, but now he was jobless, and spent most of his time with his dogs, fighting them, betting on them, and winning or losing money. Her brothers were still in school as well as her younger sisters. Her mother was a housewife. The movies she had made after *Osama* had not achieved the same high level of fame, but many were as good, and perhaps even better in some ways. They sold briskly when they showed up in Kabul's pirate DVD market.

"I've been in some Asian countries for film festivals," Marina said. "I was given a gold horse medal at one of them, but it was stolen before it actually got to me." She giggled. "I was told that it was just covered in gold, and it didn't cost that much, so not to worry about it." She giggled again.

After an hour of talking, drinking tea and making jokes, Corinne and the interpreter left, but not before asking Marina to come to the Foundation the next day for an audition.

:::::

Marina was already there waiting when Corinne arrived at the Foundation the following afternoon. Nabi Tanha and Shah Mohammed were there as well, though no one had asked them to come. They just wanted to see Corinne, say hello, and find out when the project would start. Corinne was happy to see them, and updated them. She explained that Marina was about to have an audition, and invited them to stay. Then she asked Marina to improvise anything that she was comfortable doing. Marina, however, had no idea what Corinne wanted. She did not understand the meaning of words such as "audition," "improvisation" or "rehearsal." She only knew how to stand before a camera, say a line, and make faces as she was told by the director.

When the concept of improvisation was explained to her, she said, "I'd like to do a little girl who is in search of a book that, she was told, will answer all her questions about life's mysteries: why one person is poor and one is rich, one is sick and another is healthy, and why one is sane and one is mad, and so on."

"Go ahead," Corinne said.

Before Marina started, she began to giggle and could not stop. Everyone laughed with her, but she continued giggling to the point that it became a bit tedious. She noticed that everyone else had stopped laughing. She wanted to stop giggling, but she could not. "I can't stop," she said. "When it comes, I can't stop."

Corinne did not know what to do either, or how to help her.

Nabi suggested that she should do some improvisations about her life, recounting her memories of her childhood. Corinne agreed. Immediately, a cloud swept over Marina's face as she nodded her head and grew quiet.

"I was little. Life was hard," she started. "I saw girls in nice clothes holding their parents' hands going from one shop to the next, buying beautiful clothes. I had no hands to hold on to. I had parents, but they lived at the mercy of the passersby. I learned from them how to do the same. Sometimes people gave me some food or a little money. Sometimes they were angry with me for being hungry. Sometimes they laughed at me, especially the kids.

"My feelings for those kids were mixed with happiness and jealousy. I felt happy for them because they could have everything they wanted. Yet I felt jealous towards them, because I wasn't born with the same chances. Life was a mystery to me. Why is one so poor and another can have everything? Why didn't God create everybody the same and equal?"

Suddenly, she started to cry. Her small audience thought she was acting. She tried to continue, but sobs clung to her voice as she attempted to recount one memory after another. Her face was wet with her tears, and she covered her face with her hands. Her whole body shook. Everyone felt sorry for her. She was touching something within them. She sat on the ground and put her head on her knees.

"Is she still acting?" Corinne asked the interpreter in a whisper. "She is so good."

"I don't think she is acting," he replied.

Abruptly, Corinne got up and hugged Marina. She started rubbing Marina's back, saying softly, "Shhh, shhhh. It is OK." Corinne's two daughters were nearly the same age as Marina. At that moment, Corinne understood instinctively as a mother that what Marina needed had nothing to do with being in a play. She held Marina for several minutes and let her sob against her chest.

Nabi was wiping his eyes, but not wanting anybody to see. He walked towards Marina to make jokes with her to cheer her up. Or maybe just to escape painful memories of his own. Shah Moham-med, who could always make people laugh, made some funny faces at Marina, but she could not see them through her tears.

Nabi said, "Marina, cry, cry. Crying is good for the eyes. In the West, people go to pharmacies to buy artificial tears to wash out their eyes. We have plenty of them by ourselves. We may not have a lot of clean things in Afghanistan, but our eyes are the cleanest in the world."

Marina raised her face and looked at him, wanting to believe him. Corinne rocked her back and forth until she quieted. When Marina gave a little giggle, they knew she would be all right.

"From now on," Nabi said with unusual tenderness, "I'll be your uncle, and I will protect you."

Marina smiled at him, and whispered, "*Tashekur, Kaka Nabi* [Thank you, Uncle Nabi]." Throughout the weeks that followed, Nabi took that promise seriously, and did many things to help Marina learn the craft of acting on stage.

Now the cast was completed. Marina was in. Rehearsals could start.

:::::

Corinne went home to the old fort that night filled with a sense of accomplishment. She made jokes with the interpreter all the way home. Then she told the interpreter that he was invited to dinner as a thank-you for his hard work. He accepted the invitation. Dinner with Corinne and David often meant tasting foods he had never had before. If he did not like them, he could always go downstairs and eat what his mother had made.

They entered the courtyard just as David finished picking arugula from the small garden he had planted. As they climbed the uneven mud-brick stairs to his rooms, Corinne told him about the women she had decided to cast.

"Marina will need a lot of guidance," she said as she set out some locally-made goat cheese, "but she has a quality that is absolutely electric."

"That was evident in *Osama*," David agreed, as he uncorked a bottle of chardonnay and poured glasses for Corinne and himself.

Corinne found some fancy crackers that David had bought at a store open only to foreigners and put them on the plate with the cheese. "The only one I am uncertain about is Breshna Bahar. She is very good, but I don't know whether she is too hard-edged to play a noblewoman."

"People like seeing her on TV," the interpreter reassured her as he squeezed some oranges to make himself a glass of juice.

Corinne gathered up the plates of salad David had tossed. "She's someone I'd like to get to know," she said. "She's wild."

The sky darkened and a light rain began to fall. Plans to eat out on the terrace were abandoned.

"Bring the cheese plate," she told the interpreter and followed David down two steps into a large room covered with many fine old carpets. They sat on cushions near the tall windows that they swung open wide, allowing the rain-freshened air to fill the elegant room.

Corinne told David how she had been fascinated by Saba Sahar, who seemed to be in an entirely different class from the others. She described Saba's improvisation as best she could from what the interpreter had told her. "She's good, but she wears so much makeup. She's going to have to get rid of all that if she's going to be in this show."

David stretched out his legs and nestled himself into the over-sized cushion as he took a sip of his wine.

As the interpreter put the plate of cheese on a low table in front of them, he asked Corinne, "Had you ever thought you would one day be in Kabul and directing a play by Shakespeare?"

"Had you ever thought you would one day be working for a French director?"

"But you are not a director yet, and you are not French either. You're half Kurdish and half German."

"Cheeky Afghan," Corinne sniffed, as David laughed with wine in his mouth and tried to keep from spitting it into his salad.

Rehearsals, Act One

Kabul. June 2005.

On the first day of rehearsals, the actors gathered in one of the large rooms at the Foundation and sat in a circle around the familiar Hazaragi *kilim*. All the women sat on one side of the circle, all the men on the other.

Corinne gave them each a copy of the script, and told them not to read it. She explained the story of the play, going scene by scene, bringing each of the characters to life. Then she announced who would be playing which part.

"Shah Mohammed, I'd like you to be the grandiloquent King of Kabul," she said. "Shakespeare called you Ferdinand. Choose an Afghan name for your character."

"I never expected I would be a king one day," Shah Mohammed laughed. "Why not? My name is King Haroon." Then he looked at everyone in the room and continued, "My good people, your king is at your service. But don't ask what your king can do for you. Ask yourself what you can do for your king."

"I thought I would be the king," Nabi said, a slightly petulant edge to his voice.

"I have a better role for you," Corinne said. "Shakespeare called you Biron. It is the most important role in the play."

"Is it?"

"Yes!" Corinne said encouragingly. "Your character makes all the big decisions."

The frown on Nabi's face was replaced by a self-assured smile. Then he looked at everyone in the room and said, "People, know that your king is nothing but a puppet. I'm the puppet master, and my name is Sohrab."

Now Faisal was excited to hear what role he was assigned. "Who am I? Who am I?"

"You are Faisal," Corinne said straight-faced.

Everyone laughed.

"Shakespeare called you Dumain," Corinne said.

"I prefer Mansour," Faisal said, preening.

"Why not Ahmad Zahir?" Shah Mohammed shouted out. Everyone again laughed and started singing Ahmad Zahir songs. Faisal was thrilled.

Aref was now the only nobleman left.

"Shakespeare called you Longeville," Corinne said.

"And I like the name Sherzad," Aref said. "It sounds very heroic."

"Like you," Nabi jibed.

"Yes, like me!" Aref joked back as he struck the pose of a strong man.

Then Corinne looked at Kabir Rahimi. "You are a combination of several characters who all acted as messengers, Kabir."

"Then make me Sikander," Kabir said. "Maybe I'm just a messenger, but I want the name of a conqueror." In Dari, 'Sikander' is the local variant of 'Alexander.'

"Sikander jan," chimed in Breshna, "I want to watch you conquer something." Kabir looked suddenly shy as everyone chortled.

Now Corinne turned to the girls.

Saba Sahar seemed as if she already knew she would be the princess. Everyone could see that she would be best for that role. Shakespeare had called her character the Princess of France. She changed it, though, to Princess of Herat, one of the ancient centers of learning in Afghanistan.

"Marina jan, I would like you to be Rosaline," Corinne stated.

"Whoever you think is the best for me," Marina said, and then giggled.

"What should we call her?" Corinne queried.

"I like Senober."

"That is a pretty name. All right, Breshna jan," Corinne said. "Are you happy playing Maria?"

"If she has some good lines," Breshna said. "I can do that. Change her name to Maryam, which is not so different from Maria."

"Good! That's very good," Corinne agreed as she made a note in her script. Then she turned to Leila.

"We have a princess named Katherine," Corinne said.

"All right, but I like the name Narges."

"Another good name," Corinne said.

"I thought I would be one of the princesses," Parwin protested. Then she laughed. "I'm joking. I'm fine being the lady-in-waiting to the others."

"What name would you like to call her?" Corinne asked her.

"Fatima."

"Fatima it is," Corinne said. "Now I want each of you to read your role without acting. For today, I just want all of you to get a sense of the play."

∷∷∷

Within moments, a serious problem became apparent. Only Nabi, Saba, Shah Mohammed and Aref could read the script with any ease. Some of the others could read it a little, but they had difficulty understanding the meaning of many of the words and even whole sentences.

Marina faced the greatest challenge. She could not read any of her lines. When she should have been in school, she had been out begging for food so her brothers and sisters would have something to eat. With the rudimentary reading skills she had mastered, she was completely unprepared to make sense of Shakespeare's dated vocabulary and poetic allusions.

Even the actors who had no difficulty reading were pressed to make sense of individual words. The immensity of the issue was apparent right from the opening lines of the play, spoken by Shah Mohammed as Haroon, the King of Kabul:

HAROON
Let fame, that all hunt after in their lives,
Live register'd upon our brazen tombs
And then grace us in the disgrace of death;
Kabul shall be the wonder of the world;
Our court shall be a little Academe,
Still and contemplative in living art.

Shah Mohammed read the lines slowly, then looked up with questions in his eyes. He glanced at the script once more, not sure whether to go on. He had not been able to take in the meaning of what he had just read. No one else understood his lines either. He read them again. "I understand the last three lines, but I'm not sure what Mr. Shakespeare was trying to say in the first three lines."

And so it went with the others. Breshna as Maryam was confronted with:

MARYAM
If love makes me forsworn, how shall I swear to love?
Ah, never faith could hold, if not to beauty vow'd!
Though to myself forsworn, to thee I'll faithful prove:
If knowledge be the mark, to know thee shall suffice.

"I think I understand the first two lines," Breshna said in a way that suggested that she perhaps did not. Marina as Senober had some of the most complex lines:

SENOBER
They are worse fools to purchase mocking so.
That same Sohrab I'll torture ere I go:
How I would make him fawn and beg and seek
And wait the season and observe the times

And spend his prodigal wits in bootless rhymes
And shape his service wholly to my hests.

When Nabi read the lines to her, she looked at him blankly.

"This is hard!" she said. The words she was hearing simply did not mean anything to her. The rest of the group read their lines and looked at each other as if they were reading another language. They understood some of the words, but they had never heard those words put together this way before.

"Come on, guys," Nabi said. "It is so poetic and beautiful."

"Is it?" Marina asked doubtfully. "It doesn't make any sense to me."

:::::

It was a full week before the cast finished reading through the whole script just once. Nabi assumed the role of mentor and helped the others understand their lines. Sometimes Saba and Shah Mohammed did so as well, but they spent most of their free time studying their own lines. They walked around the room or out on the lawn, and said their lines to the trees and rosebushes as if they were the other players on the stage, who would say their own lines back to them.

Corinne was anxious to be doing more than watching the actors read. Without knowing Dari, however, she could not easily be part of their conversations about the script. Her frustration was evident. From time to time, she would interrupt them, ask what they were talking about and beg them to move things along a little faster. They said that they would try. But they could not.

:::::

After one week, the actual rehearsing began. The actors sat in a circle. As always, all the men were on one side, and all the women on the other. Every day, Corinne tried to get them to mix, but no one moved. The younger women did not look at the men even when they were speaking to them. Corinne joked about that with them, and prodded, but had little success getting them to make eye contact with the men.

"What am I going to have to do to get you to mix together?" she asked.

No one answered. She made a mental note to work on breaking down their resistance, but she had too much else to do just then to focus on it at that moment.

The actors started reading the play aloud, with a lot of stumbling over the strange words. Corinne sometimes interrupted to encourage them to speak louder, to project their voices. When she found that the actors could not do it properly, she taught them vocal exercises.

Once, when Nabi was having a problem reading an especially troublesome word, his voice dropped. Corinne stopped him, saying, "We have to pronounce the words forcefully, and not as if we're reading them for ourselves. Pretend you're onstage reading for hundreds of people in the audience and …"

Nabi, who did not welcome being interrupted, mumbled, "I think she is the kind of woman who interferes too much in other people's affairs. I don't know if we can manage to stay and work with her."

Corinne seemed to sense the discontent, and stopped speaking. Saba took Corinne's silence as an opportunity to offer advice to Nabi. "Don't judge someone by their words," she told him. "Consider what people think of you, not what they say. She thinks well of you. She came all the way from the West to tell you something of her work, which is respected there. You have to combine the understanding of the East, and the knowledge of the West that she brought with her. What she tells you is for the play, and it is good to know."

Nabi rolled his eyes as if he did not want to be lectured.

"She has a good eye for details, such as how you should be speaking," Saba continued. "A director has to notice things, often very little things in order to find the right move for the scene and remove all the mistakes. And a director's eyes are like a camera, always taking photographs in their mind and always trying to understand what is going on."

"Enough of your philosophy," Nabi said dismissively.

Saba was not intimidated. She replied, "I would be on your side if you were right."

Corinne quietly asked the interpreter with disquiet in her voice, "Do I need to know what the hell is going on?"

Nabi, who understood English, whispered to the interpreter in Dari, "Don't tell her what I said. Just tell her that Saba made me understand better."

"Well ... nothing special," the interpreter diplomatically replied to Corinne. "Saba explained exactly the same thing that you just said. That is all."

Corinne unleashed her frustration of the past week on the interpreter. "Why did she have to do that? Didn't you interpret everything properly? Why didn't Nabi understand what I said? You really have to listen carefully, and tell them exactly what I say. Otherwise it'll all be a mess. I don't need two translators. One translator is enough."

The interpreter did not know what to say. He needed the small money he was being paid, so he said quietly, "Yes. I will try."

Every day, there were moments like that. Corinne could not stop the actors from arguing among themselves over things she had told them. When the interpreter tried to translate what they were saying to Corinne, they whispered, "Don't tell her. Say something else."

∷∷∷

Finally, the actors were on their feet. Corinne was working out their positions with them. Some moved a bit clumsily, though, and Corinne had to explain basic techniques, such as not blocking the audience's view of the other actors.

Marina was still puzzled about what theater was. One day she asked, "Why bother with theater? Why not make a movie? It is easy to make, easy to buy in shops and easy for anyone to watch any time they want to watch it."

She was hardworking, but was having a difficult time. She had more lines than either Leila or Breshna, and in the first weeks whenever it was time for her to speak, she looked at everyone in wide-eyed fear before opening her mouth. When she spoke, she had pronunciation problems. And when she had to look at the script, she had reading problems. She had crying problems a few times. Sometimes she had giggling problems. When she started giggling, no one could stop her because everything seemed funny to her, until something reminded her of the Taliban times or the war. And then no one could stop her crying.

One day Marina asked, "Was Shakespeare a Talib kind of guy? Why is he so strict with all these rules?"

Saba explained to Marina that Shakespeare had died four hundred years ago, long before the Taliban. She giggled for a moment, then her eyes moistened briefly before she started giggling again.

As the weeks passed, she nonetheless became a much-loved and much-respected member of the company. Marina was never late, or sick, or complaining. She was always in good spirits, always trying her best to do a good job. There is a saying in Dari: "She has a back for work." Also, small acts of kindness were part of her every day. When she had a quiet moment, she took it upon herself to look after Parwin's daughter, Shogufa. Or she would help the Foundation staff in some way. She was happy to be in the company of the other actors. They could feel that, and they returned her good feelings.

::::::

Earlier in the summer, the Foundation had built a stage at one end of its garden. It was used every weekend for concerts of classical

Afghan music, and Robert planned to make it the main stage for the upcoming Afghan Theater Festival. For *Love's Labour's Lost*, though, Corinne wanted to perform in the center of the garden, with the audience seated around the actors on three sides. Most of the action would take place on carpets laid out in the grass.

The raised stage, however, had about the same amount of playing area as the actors would be using on the grass, so they started rehearsing on it. They would start their rehearsals in the grand salon, often reading through the scenes they planned to rehearse, then move out to the stage in the garden. When they climbed its three steps, something about them changed. It was as if they were leaving Kabul and entering Shakespeare's world. From the moment Aref stepped onto the stage, he became a young noble. Saba became a princess.

As Corinne moved around the stage with the actors, guiding them to their positions and explaining their movements, she was more relaxed than she had been in the previous weeks when she had been forced to sit and wait for the actors to work their way through the script. That frustration had given way to the kind of dynamism that comes from doing something creative. She became the funny and happy Corinne again, and that made everyone else relax as well.

Corinne worked closely with the women. She took into account what they did not know or could not do, and looked for ways to help them use the skills they had. She was especially gentle with Leila and Marina, even when they made mistakes. Saba kept her distance from Corinne personally, but she understood Corinne professionally, and did what was asked without any argument, and did it well.

Breshna was like a human tornado, often twisting her lines in ways that threw the others off. Corinne would be unhappy with the others, not knowing what had caused the problem. There would then be about five minutes of backing-and-forthing with the interpreter in the middle trying to straighten things out. The actors' voices would start rising, and Corinne's voice would deepen. That was her serious voice. Then Breshna would crack a joke that made all the actors burst out laughing, and everyone would go on to the next thing, with Corinne looking confused but content.

Rehearsals, Act Two

Kabul. July 2005.

When the actors held discussions during their breaks, they said so much so quickly that the interpreter could not translate everything. Corinne knew she was missing a lot, and that left her frustrated. So she often used the break time to go over paperwork with Robert or to make phone calls. She was keenly interested, though, to hear what the actors were thinking. When the interpreter explained on the ride home who had said what, she was unhappy because she would have liked to have added something at the time.

Her mind never stopped thinking about the play, even as she was cooking or washing the spices and greens that David brought in from his garden. Sometimes she invited the interpreter to eat with them. While they talked, she taught him how to make the dressing for the salad. When he came for dinner the next time, he knew what to do.

Sometimes they ate around the table in the kitchen with candles. Sometimes they went to the terrace with their plates and sat on the steps. They talked about all kinds of things, but mostly Corinne asked the interpreter about the actors' personal lives. She wanted to know them better.

:::::

Breshna had been more open about her life outside the play than most of the others. One day she mentioned that she had lost her husband to an artillery round in 1992 during the civil war. When Corinne had asked if hers had been an arranged marriage, Breshna had shaken her head wistfully. It was on a day when Breshna had been the first actor to arrive and only Corinne and the interpreter were at the Foundation. They sat in the garden sipping green tea and chatting.

"My husband and I arranged ourselves," she said with her hearty laugh. "We were a love match." They had two daughters in their dozen years together.

"One of my daughters is married and has a son," she said.

"You look much too young to be a grandmother," Corinne said.

Breshna shrugged. "Now I'm living with my mother and my younger daughter," she said, deflecting Corinne's comment, "along with the two nephews – the sons of my brother who was killed. They are like sons to me."

In Taliban times, she had gone hungry, Breshna said matter-of-factly. Now she was a policewoman, earning extra money by working in films and driving her own car. The fame that had come with her television career, though, was sometimes a burden.

"Whenever I go out, people call at me, 'Gul Chera, how is your husband, Bulbul?' That makes me miss my own husband. Bulbul is my husband only in the TV series, and they know he is not my real husband. I feel I'm being insulted. But I smile, and say nothing. I smile in my face, and cry in my heart.

"I got so sick of everybody calling me Gul Chera that I started wearing a *burqa* when I had to go somewhere and I was not driving. One day I got into a taxi and told the driver where he should take me. He turned and asked, "Are you Gul Chera?" He'd recognized my voice. I stopped wearing the *burqa* after that."

:::::

The actors rehearsed the scenes in order. The first scene was with only the boys. They were beginning to show what each of them could do. Nabi Tanha commanded the playing area marked out in the grand salon just by the way he moved. He knew where to place himself to create visual relationships between himself and the other actors. When he spoke, his words were clear, and always as if he were saying them for the first time.

Nabi often made suggestions to Shah Mohammed on how he should play his scenes. Shah Mohammed would look off in the distance while Nabi was speaking, then nod his head, and do what had been suggested.

One thing for which Shah Mohammed needed no help was speaking clearly. His enunciation was a joy to hear as he always pronounced his words precisely and poetically.

Aref surprised everyone. From the first time that he spoke his lines, all the other actors stopped what they were doing and listened to him. He was like a magnet and had the gift of making people pay close attention to him.

Faisal watched the other three closely. He was creative and full of suggestions on how everyone should be playing their scenes. Corinne listened to his ideas at first, but he had so many. As the clock ticked down to the end of a rehearsal and his ideas kept coming, Corinne got exasperated. Faisal just smiled and said, "Take it easy, *Khanom-e-zelzela* [Madame Earthquake], it was just an idea." The others snickered. The interpreter told Corinne, "He said, 'It was just an idea.'"

"When I need an idea," Corinne replied with a sigh as she looked for her place in the script, "I will ask for one. But not every time I give him some direction."

::::::

The second scene was with the girls. From the first rehearsal to the last performance, Saba Sahar was a one-person rescue squad among the girls, ready to assist anyone in trouble. With a half-smile, a slight raising of her eyebrow or a tilt of her head, she could help the others remember a line, or guide them to move to some place they had forgotten to go.

Breshna Bahar had energy and good instincts. She seemed to learn more through trial and error than by taking direction.

Even after Marina and Leila began to understand the individual words, they fought to grasp the full meanings of the sentences. Corinne worked out movements for them to go with their lines. Since they could make no sense of the lines, they quickly forgot what she intended them to do.

This became a real problem when the actors reached the third scene, when the boys and the girls were on stage together for the first time. Marina, as Senober, had a quick exchange with Sohrab. That went well, but in the next piece of dialogue between the two of them, Sohrab said:

SOHRAB
Lady, I will commend you to mine own heart.

SENOBER
Pray you, do my commendations; I would be glad to see it.

Marina understood that Sohrab was leaving, but was confused when Corinne was unhappy with the gesture she had made as he went, as if she were dismissing a pushcart-man. Corinne tried to help her find a different kind of gesture more suited for a noble-woman. They spent a long time on this. Marina was at a loss, though, when it came to putting the newly devised gesture together with the line that was little more than random sounds to her.

In Afghanistan, with its many languages, it is common for people not to understand what someone next to them is saying. Often people learn a few functional phrases of another language – "thank you", "goodbye", "how much" – even if they do not know the precise meaning of each word. Marina was working in this kind of linguistic borderland, doing the best she could, intuitively presuming that, over time, these odd sounds would start to make sense to her. In the meantime, her lines could have as easily been in Turkmeni, Pashayi, Uzbeki or some other of Afghanistan's twenty-two languages.

One day in exasperation, she asked, "Why do I have to talk to Sohrab so poetically? Instead of asking him if his soul suffers, why can't I say, 'Are you in pain?'"

While Marina struggled and Corinne explained, the others got bored. The smokers had to smoke. Corinne hated the smell. She interrupted her discussion with Marina to complain about it strenuously. "How many times do I have to tell you not to smoke in the room?"

"Where do you want us to smoke then?" the actors shot back at her, usually several of them together.

"Outside."

"We don't have time to finish half a cigarette," one smoker moaned, "before you ask us to come back. What is the point of going outside?"

"You are here to rehearse, not to smoke."

"Then let's start!" the actors demanded.

The interpreter tried to move things along to the next scene so the fussing would not become a brawl.

:::::

Corinne and the interpreter talked many times about Marina's and Leila's difficulties. "They still don't grasp the meaning of their lines, do they?" she said with concern one afternoon as they headed to the Foundation to rehearse.

"No," he replied. "And I don't think they understand many of the lines the other actors are saying to them, either."

"I guessed that," Corinne replied.

"That's why they keep missing their cues."

"Maybe I should cut some of their lines," Corinne suggested.

She did. When that failed to help, she undid the cuts and began working separately with Leila and Marina each day before the rest of the actors arrived. She asked them to explain *Love's Labour's Lost* in their own words, in simple storytelling. At first, they were at a complete loss. Every day they worked on a different scene. It was slow going with no sure indication as to how much Leila and Marina were internalizing.

One thing that did seem to help them was the daily routine of hearing the other actors read their lines aloud very fast without acting them. Corinne interrupted from time to time and asked them explain the meaning of the lines they had just read. Leila and Marina began to understand how their parts fitted in with everyone else's. However, they still had problems.

∴∴∴

At the beginning of the third week of rehearsals, Corinne decided it was time to get the men and women interacting. They still came in every day and took their places on opposite sides of the grand salon. So just before the tea break, Corinne led the way out to the garden and asked the actors to form a large circle on the grass. As usual, all the women were on one side and all the men on the other. Corinne handed a soccer ball to Nabi and told him, "You have to throw it to someone in the circle, but that person must be of the opposite gender."

"All right," Nabi said as he tossed the ball to Marina.

"OK, Marina, now you have to throw it to one of the boys," Corinne instructed. "Fast, fast, fast!" Marina heaved the ball to Aref, who threw it back to Breshna. Slowly, shyness gave way to laughter as the ball flew back and forth for several minutes.

"Now before you throw the ball to the other person," Corinne interrupted, "You have to call his or her name and make eye contact as you do."

This made the exercise a little more challenging, especially for the girls. Leila forgot to call out the boys' names. Marina still could not make eye contact. For all that, though, they were laughing and enjoying the game, even if they were not feeling entirely comfortable doing it.

∴∴∴

The weather kept getting hotter. The actors could no longer work indoors. Neither the grand salon nor any of the Foundation's other rooms had air conditioning. The group moved outside, but the sun on the stage in the garden was scorching. Everyone started getting cranky, the way people do in Kabul when the heat and dust rises and there is no good air to breathe. Then, every day one of the actors fell sick, either from food poisoning or dehydration. At one time or another, everyone had diarrhea. Even Corinne. That is life in Kabul.

From the first rehearsal, Corinne had become steadily more annoyed that her sessions at the Foundation could not start until 4:00 PM when those who had jobs were free. She grew upset when actors arrived late. There was not a single day when everyone came on time. The actors merely shrugged their shoulders and said, "Traffic jam."

"I was not feeling well."

"Traffic jam."

"We had some guests, and I had to make them tea."

"Traffic jam."

"I had a lot of school work."

"Traffic jam."

"I had to cook lunch for my father."

"Traffic jam."

"We had a lot of work in the office."

"Traffic jam."

"I went to see a doctor, and here is my medicine."

"Traffic jam."

Corinne arranged for her driver Daoud to pick up Marina and Leila and get them to the Foundation on time. Saba and Breshna drove their own cars and were at the mercy of the traffic. Parwin came on her own from a distant part of Kabul far from Daoud's route. Corinne implored the men to come when they were supposed to. Most did, but not always.

She could work with the actors only until 6:30 PM, or at the latest to 7:00 PM. The women had to be home before dark or their neighbors would start gossiping about them. In Afghanistan, a woman is either a "good woman," which means she does what her husband or family expects her to do, or she is not. There are few gradations in between.

With such a short time to rehearse every day, Corinne became more and more anxious. She had not expected to need a full week to get the actors through the first reading of the script. She had had no way of understanding how complicated and time-consuming it would be to work through an interpreter.

She was always wanting to say something to the actors. The actors were always wanting to say something in return. Sometimes Corinne spoke insistently, trying to convey the urgency of the situation in her tone of voice. The actors did not understand her words until they had been translated, but they heard the edge in her voice, and bristled at it. Perhaps this was the way directors worked in France, they grumbled to each other, but in Afghanistan we have rules for how people speak to one another.

Impatient to move the rehearsal along, and not understanding when Nabi was suggesting something helpful about a scene, Corinne would habitually cut him off midsentence. The next minute, Nabi would walk out of the rehearsal, and encourage Shah Mohammed and Faisal to leave too. He was their leader. They generally did as he did. This happened several times. Corinne would look at the interpreter pleadingly, asking him to find a way to get them to come back. The interpreter would take a deep breath, pump himself up with a manufactured positive energy and go out into the dusty street as they were walking away. He would beg them to come back, while Corinne busied herself with the girls.

"Do you know the reason for my quitting?" Nabi argued.

"No," the interpreter said each time, even though he knew exactly what Nabi was going to say next.

"Tell her that this is not how we talk in this part of the world. We listen to one another, even if we know that the other person is completely wrong, and then we express our ideas and thoughts in a polite and respectful manner. We don't cut people off while they are speaking. If she were a man, I would have smashed her face by now."

"All right," the interpreter would reply in a consoling voice. "Please come back. We're running out of time." And one way or another he managed to soothe Nabi's feelings and bring him back. And with him came Shah Mohammed and Faisal, who had not really wanted to leave anyway.

Sometimes Parwin had to help get Nabi Tanha back. She could always find the right words to say. "Nabi jan, don't be angry with Corinne," she would say. "She is one of those people who talks first, then thinks about what she just said. Have you heard of the expression, 'Your mouth is your best friend if you have control of it, and your worst enemy if you don't?' Her mouth may be an enemy to her, but she means well."

Nabi listened to Parwin because she was the second oldest among the actors in a society where age brings respect. In a tight voice, however, he always warned the interpreter, "You have to teach Corinne some manners when you have dinner with her."

"All right, Nabi jan," the interpreter always assured him. "I will. I promise."

:·:·:·:

Breshna quit about once a week, saying in English, "I don't want to do this. It doesn't worth it." She complained that she was being paid very little for all this irritation, even though the actors were each receiving $600, which was a lot more than most of them were making in their jobs.

On such occasions, the interpreter argued, "Breshna jan, a true actor does not care for the money, but for art and quality. You are performing Shakespeare here. Not every actor can do Shakespeare, not even famous ones." This inevitably worked, and she came back.

:·:·:·:

What Corinne only slowly began to understand was that all the Afghans involved in the play, and, in fact, everyone in Afghanistan, was under endless stress from the moment they woke up in the morning until they went to bed. Even then, their stress did not ease. Would a bomb explode during the night? Would a telephone call come about a relative who has been killed? Would it be safe to send the children to school in the morning? It never stopped. They had been living like this for almost thirty years, longer than the younger actors had been alive.

When the interpreter took the actors aside, he gave them a moment of quiet and calm where they could release their anger at the lives they were being forced to live. Maybe they would shout about something Corinne had said to them that they did not like, but really they just had to vent about something – anything – because everything else had become too much.

They all wanted to be in the play. They all wanted to be good actors. They all wanted to learn what Corinne could teach them. They all knew that they had to let go of what had ignited their anger and return to the rehearsal.

Perhaps the heart of the issue may have been Corinne's astonishing drive. Even when the actors were sitting quietly under a pomegranate tree in the Foundation's garden before a rehearsal, they always knew when Corinne had arrived. A special kind of energy seemed to move ahead of her. She was not noisy or trying to attract attention. It was just that the air changed and became charged when she entered. Sometimes, though, this single-minded forcefulness seemed to act like a spark that unintentionally sets off an explosion.

Corinne once asked if they had a problem with a woman giving orders. Maybe this was true for the men on some level, but it was not an issue for the women, and some of them quit more often than the men.

:::::

Corinne tried to help the actors understand what she wanted from them. They could all see that she was a good teacher, and often said so. If only everyone had spoken the same language, it would have been easier. There were times when Corinne could not find the right words to explain something to the actors, and she would run out of patience and walk away. She would come back after ten minutes, and start again. There were a couple of times near the end of the day when she became completely fed up, and just left the Foundation and went home, leaving the interpreter in charge. On the way back to the fort, she would call the interpreter and ask him to help the actors work on their lines.

It was clear that Corinne's mind was racing with ideas she wanted to share, while the actors were discovering this curious world of Shakespeare at a very different pace. Corinne was on a deadline. The actors were on a journey of discovery.

Tea with Shakespeare

Kabul. June and July 2005.

The limited time for rehearsing each day was made even shorter because of a half-hour break at 5:00 PM to drink tea and eat cake and cookies that the Foundation provided.

The tea breaks gave the actors an opportunity to talk among themselves. A frequent topic was Shakespeare. So much about him was new to them. Just being in a play was new to several of them. Many of the actors were new to each other. Their discussions, which occasionally grew surprisingly heated, were a time of discovery for all.

One day as he was pouring the tea, Shah Mohammed asked the group, "Who wants to share his impressions of Shakespeare?" Shah Mohammed had a way of relating to the group as if he were everyone's favorite uncle.

At first, no one replied to his suggestion. Then, Nabi Tanha responded like a thoughtful and well-educated mullah. He drew himself up and started moving his hands in graceful arcs to amplify his points. "Shakespeare brings utter silence into your consciousness." Nabi, who usually talked in the Kabul street dialect, was matching the language of his gestures with formal and poetic Dari. He raised his eyebrows to emphasize the points he thought were important.

He went on, "The way Shakespeare uses words, they rush like a small river from somewhere far away, and bring sadness and happiness, restlessness and restfulness into you. They make you feel sorry for yourself and everyone else, and vice versa. His poetry leaves you motionless, and takes you into a deep, thoughtful silence." Nabi was crouched between a kneeling and squatting position. His thin, expressive body was becoming a part of what he was saying. The others watched him, sipping their tea.

"When I read Shakespeare's lines," Nabi went on, "I want to glue my eyes to each verse until I become blind. I want to take in every part of every word and know all its meanings." He relaxed back onto his *toshak*. "However, I don't think our people will understand Shakespeare. Shakespeare plays with words and ideas, while our people played with guns for the past three decades. Some days, I think that doing Shakespeare is a waste of time."

Saba looked at Nabi with cool-eyed approval. "You're very insightful," she told him, "even more than I thought. However, I won't let you tell us that 'doing Shakespeare is a waste of time.' People in this country understood Shakespeare thirty years ago. Why can't they do so now? Do we go forward or backward?" She adjusted her headscarf, which had the effect of focusing attention on her large, carefully made-up dark eyes, and continued. "You have to think of the words you say before they come out of your mouth, and ask yourself if they're worth saying. You judge very quickly without taking the time to think things through, like these crazy politicians we have. You can see the result of their wrong judgments in all these years of war."

Saba spoke with the directness of someone who is accustomed to people paying attention to what she says. She went on, "We have to believe that our obligation is to replace guns with words. These wars in our country were made by dangerously narrow-minded people who preferred weapons over words. We have to think that human nature can be improved. Guns kill you. Words can save you."

Nabi had been challenged, and was ready to fight. Shah Mohammed saw that, and tried to tamp things down before they erupted. "Enough out of both of you," he said. "Are you going to give the rest of us a chance to talk?"

Saba eyed him with an air of jovial superiority and prodded him, saying, "I will shut up, if you have anything to say that is worth hearing."

Shah Mohammed smiled and replied, "All I wanted to say was let's drink our tea before it gets cool. I'm hungry. I want to eat, and I'm waiting for you and Nabi jan to start so I may. Instead, you two accelerated like a car with no brakes that no one can stop." Everyone laughed, and the crisis was diffused.

:::::

There were many, many more discussions about Shakespeare during the breaks. It was a time when the actors felt free to express themselves. Being Afghans, they spoke at some length. Being Afghans, everyone enjoyed listening to the others, and then replying at some length.

Nabi often initiated the conversations. He had emerged as the strongest member of the group, though Saba and Breshna would probably not agree with that. Indeed, they rarely agreed with Nabi on anything.

One day Nabi turned to Kabir Rahimi, the quiet one, and asked him what he thought of *Love's Labour's Lost*. Kabir started by saying, "Shakespeare was an artist of words, and he loved his art with all his being. I can see that. Maybe you can as well. That is why when I read his plays, his poetry rises into my heart and brings a kind of feeling to me that I can't explain."

Everyone was quiet and interested in hearing what Kabir had to say. Not only was he the oldest member of the group, and thus deserving of their respect, he was not by nature a talker. He smiled a lot, but said little. He went on, "By listening to Shakespeare, those with guilty consciences suffer. If you suffer from a wound, it can be healed. If you suffer with your conscience, it cannot. He knew that."

Kabir spoke with confidence. There was a hint of worry in his eyes, however, lest the insights that Shakespeare had given him, and which he found precious, would be dismissed by the others.

He kept on speaking, though. "The wounds that we suffered in all of the fighting here, they will be forgotten in a few years. By doing this play, we will bring our suffering to those with guilty consciences who are still in this country and ruling us. That is why we must invite them, the warlords. In fact, we can change our visible wounds to invisible wounds that hurt from the inside out."

This was the most the group had ever heard Kabir say. No one wanted to say anything after he had spoken. They all sipped their tea for a few minutes and kept quiet. Kabir retreated into his teacup and said no more.

Nabi was intent on keeping the conversation going, though, and he turned to Aref.

"I didn't know much about Shakespeare before I came here," Aref responded. "I'm learning so much about him and his work every day. Each time I read something that Shakespeare has written, I get the feeling that I understand everything that he is saying. The next day, though, I discover something else in those same verses that I didn't know the day before. And the next day, one more thing."

Aref was powerfully built and agile. Often, before rehearsals, he flexed his legs in unexpected ways, stretching like an athlete before a sporting event. His voice had a melodic quality that invited listeners in. He continued, "Shakespeare's words bring a warm light into my heart, and he charms me with his tales. His storytelling kills all my life's sorrows, and surrounds me with soft arms which bring joy. Sometimes I feel puzzled. I ask myself how such a man existed four hundred years ago? How come we don't have more like him now?"

Then he looked at everyone listening to him and said, "You know, we are dead even though we are alive. If we die tomorrow, or after a week, no one will talk about us anymore or remember us for long. Shakespeare is still alive, however, because of his plays. If I manage to write a play like his one day, I could die the next minute and be very happy. It is a big ambition, but he cannot scare Afghans from having big visions."

Shah Mohammed was beaming with approval at Aref's words. "Well done, Aref jan!" he exulted.

"Wah, wah, wah, wah ..." Faisal said in the Afghan way of showing approval or agreement.

Nabi looked around. "Who else?" he asked. "One of the ladies should talk now. Marina Golbahari! What do you think of this play and Shakespeare?"

Marina appeared startled to be asked. She was the youngest among them, and had expected all the older ones to speak first. With all the eyes looking at her, she started speaking. "I don't think I have anything worth saying," she said shyly. "When I read Shakespeare, all of a sudden I find his lines are many colors. Some are red ones or green ones or black ones and many other colors."

Marina's face was like a fast-changing sky, with sunshine one moment, and dark clouds an instant later. "I'm trying hard to understand them. When I find myself unable to read them, they pinch me, and bite me, and sting me, and make me want to cry. I don't cry, because it'll make everyone uncomfortable and unhappy. So I giggle." And she did.

Parwin looked at Marina. "We won't let these words bite or sting you, Marina jan," she said. "We'll help you understand the colors. You can just ask us when you don't know the meanings."

Marina grew calm as she felt the goodness radiating from Parwin.

Nabi was nodding. Marina, perhaps because she was so young, was especially shy when talking to the men. Ever since Nabi had encouraged her to call him uncle, the tension that kept her shoulders tight had eased when she was talking with him. After she had been coming to rehearsals for a week or so, he had told her that Shah Mohammed and Faisal were like brothers to him. If they were his brothers, then that meant that they, too, were her uncles, and she should feel at ease with them. Slowly, she accepted them, but she would quickly tighten up again when she had to speak to the other men.

Nabi Tanha leaned towards Parwin as he spoke to her, saying, "You give Marina good advice, Parwin jan. Now it is your turn to tell us what you think. We've been working for all these weeks now, yet we haven't heard a word from you. At least tell us why you're doing this play, for the play's beauty or for the money?"

Everyone chuckled. Parwin blushed. "Nabi jan, will we be rich when we do this play?" she asked. The chuckles broke into big laughs that ceased as Parwin continued in a serious voice. "I'm here for two reasons. First, it is my career choice to be an actress and to be here. Secondly, I'm very excited to do such a great play. I've never had this chance before. I find Shakespeare full of distractions, of distances, of borders and of encumbrances, more than all the other playwrights I've read. He understands everything about the human mind. Even though most of his plays are fables about royalty, he always comes back to real life, and prefers the ordinary. His message is: 'Honesty.' It is a simple message, though it takes time to understand him. You have to find the deeper meaning of his ideas."

Like Kabir, Parwin was a quiet person and rarely spoke so openly. Absent-mindedly, she looked around the garden for her young daughter, Shogufa, whom she always brought with her to rehearsals. She could leave her son at a kindergarten, but she had no one at home to care for her daughter. The little girl was well-behaved. She was sitting under a pomegranate tree, watching everyone with big eyes.

As soon as Parwin registered that Shogufa was all right, she continued. "To cut a long story short, Shakespeare has a truth that you cannot hide. He has a truth you can never forget. When our audience sees us perform Love's Labour's Lost, they will be surprised at the rhythm in his poetry. And they will find the answer to many of their unanswered questions in his verses." Parwin was a person with deep thoughts, even though she did not share them often.

Nabi turned the conversation to his sparring partner, Saba, who lit a cigarette and inhaled slowly before she spoke. Only a strong woman would smoke a cigarette outside her home, or even inside it. She was letting everyone know that she saw herself as being as important as Nabi within the group. She blew her smoke into the air as she carefully chose her words.

"Shakespeare brings caravans of ideas to his audiences," she said. "He is the best at capturing the fragrance of life, even if it is sour. His deeper message is for those who lack imaginations, who are sick with a poverty of thought and yet are in power." She inhaled again and puffed out the smoke. "I've found *Love's Labour's Lost* to be the story of narrow-minded people who impose huge limitations on everyone, with no ultimate benefit to anyone. This play is very clear in showing that putting limitations on our lives is like building a huge wall in the middle of a road on which all the people must travel to go anywhere, as the Taliban did. Sooner or later, though, that wall will be knocked down. People will force their way past the limitations, even if it costs them their lives."

Saba had an important job with the Ministry of the Interior, though she never told them what it was. She had once mentioned that she had been trained to jump out of airplanes with a parachute, without telling them why. A few times she had talked about visits to other countries for meetings representing the ministry, as well as for her film and television work. She also referred to her three children once or twice and said that she had to take care of her house like any other woman. She did not share anything with anyone about her private life, even though she also had a very public life as an actress.

One day she joked about the dark makeup she always wore around her eyes. She said, "I can act like a princess or a servant. It doesn't matter to me, it is my job to do both. But I don't want anyone to touch my makeup!" Then she laughed and asked Shah Mohammed to give his opinions on Shakespeare.

Shah Mohammed rocked forward and backward a few times. "First of all, I have to say that when the wind moves like a comb through a field of wheat, it leaves a hundred trails. Shakespeare is like a strong wind that goes direct into the human mind and conscience, and stirs up answers that we have been seeking."

Everyone nodded in agreement. Shah Mohammed's face became animated when he spoke. His mop of dark hair added to the drama of his words as he turned his head to look intently first at one person, then another. He went on, "Shakespeare can describe the cruelty of this world by making someone a prince or a princess, then showing how ignorant these people are. Then he illustrates that being ordinary can be much worthier, maybe even easier. He tells us, 'Don't yearn to be wealthy or well-known, because those things may bring unhappiness.' The deepest message in this play is: let's enjoy every colorful season, the golden earth and the blue sky, and listen to our hearts, not to our negative emotions and feelings. If you conquer the whole world, it means nothing. If you conquer your heart, though, it is everything. Life has two faces. One that laughs, and another that cries. We must strive to show the first face." Indeed, that was how Shah Mohammed approached life himself.

Saba raised her eyebrows with an impish smile, and said to him, "I'm glad you're more optimistic than your friend," meaning Nabi.

Nabi ignored her. Instead he looked around and asked, "Who's left? Oh, Faisal! You should have spoken to us before everyone else. You're our poet. Tell us your thoughts on *Love's Labour's Lost.*"

Faisal always looked to his left before he spoke, then cleared his throat like a mullah as if he were about to start a sermon. "In a roundabout way, *Love's Labour's Lost* makes fun of our recent history, the Taliban, who ruled us with their nonsense and cruel laws and regulations." Faisal kept a fuzz of whiskers. Maybe he was trying to be ready if the Taliban came back. "All these fancy words, though, in *Love's Labour's Lost* are beyond the understanding of our people. Look at us, we barely understand them ourselves."

"I disagree," Saba challenged Faisal.

"I know you do," Faisal shot back with a glint in his eye.

Everyone laughed, with Nabi laughing harder and louder than the rest.

"We have to help our audiences understand that each word has many meanings," Faisal went on. "We have to be extremely clear without changing the text. First, Shakespeare's way of using words is not our way. Secondly, we are not as educated as he was. Thirdly, we as actors have never had such a difficult text. At least I haven't.

Personally, I have never faced such a strong playwright, who can admire someone at the beginning of a sentence and destroy him at the end of it with just one word."

Nabi looked pleased.

Faisal continued, "From the first day until now, we've been getting better every day. We have to make sure that Marina and Leila understand their lines, so they can make our audiences understand them. Otherwise, a tiny mistake by one of us will cause distractions for the rest of us. I have a suggestion: someone must come every day thirty minutes early and help them understand their lines. Who will volunteer to do this?"

Everyone started explaining why he or she could not.

Nabi looked at the interpreter and said, "That only leaves you. Maybe you should do it." He knew that on many days the interpreter came early to the Foundation to enjoy the garden; his family had once had one like it, until it was destroyed in the war. Those quiet moments were supposed to be the interpreter's time for himself, but like the actors he wanted Marina and Leila to do well. So he agreed. From then on, he tutored them for one hour before the rehearsal. Day by day Marina and Leila grasped a better understanding of what Shakespeare wanted them to say.

Sometimes the interpreter took Marina and Leila to a small restaurant in Shahr-e-Naw Park, which had a private garden. The interpreter held the script like a school teacher, and asked the girls to say their lines. In between mouthfuls of pomegranate or melon ice cream, he guided them to make sense of the strange words. Breshna's daughter Wajma, who was close to Marina and Leila in age but had had more education, joined them often, and helped them when they stumbled.

Corinne nervously monitored their progress. Opening night was in less than three weeks, and they were nowhere close to being ready for it.

::::::

One evening when the rehearsal was over, Shah Mohammad invited the interpreter to his house for dinner. The interpreter could not say, "No," because it is rude to reject an invitation. After Daoud had dropped Corinne at the fort and then Marina and Leila at their homes, he took the interpreter to Shah Mohammed's house in Khair Khana.

The interpreter suggested that Daoud join them.

"I can't," Daoud replied with regret. "I have a mustache."

"What are you talking about?" the interpreter asked.

"I think that Shah Mohammed's wife and daughters will be uncomfortable around me because of my mustache."

"What?" Sometimes the interpreter had a hard time understanding Daoud's jokes.

"A mustache make a man look old. Old means I have to be wise. If I don't sound wise, Shah Mohammed's family will have a bad impression of me."

"Why don't you just get rid of your mustache?"

"Oh, no! I can't do that," he started stroking it with his right hand as his left hand remained on the wheel. He looked as if he was born to do nothing but stroke his moustache. "If I shave it, then I'll lose all my wishes." He was referring to an old fable about a lion who had six whiskers. An angel told him that if he ever got into any trouble, he could pull out one of his whiskers and the angel would be there to save him. The lion did not believe it. One day just for fun, he pulled out one of his whiskers, and the angel stood in front of him and asked what she could do for him. The lion laughed. He said he was just trying to see if it worked. Then he wasted his other five whiskers foolishly until one day he fell in a deep ditch and could not get out. He had no whisker to pull to get help, and he died.

Now Daoud continued stroking the ends of his mustache and continued, "These whiskers should be here. I may need them. You never know when the Taliban may return. They always want men to have a full beard. I can just hide at home for one week, and my beard will be as thick as my moustache. There you go! I'll be safe and can go out and be a driver."

They reached Shah Mohammed's house. As Daoud stopped to let the interpreter out, he said, "I prefer to keep my whiskers over some delicious dinner."

Shah Mohammed greeted the interpreter at the front gate, then led him upstairs to his family's apartment on the second floor. He introduced him to his wife, his five daughters and to his four-year-old son. The two men settled on *toshaks* and leaned against embroidered pillows as one of the daughters spread a white tablecloth on the floor. Another daughter put the silver basin in front of her father and poured warm water from the pitcher over his hands then passed him a small towel before doing the same for the interpreter. Meanwhile, the little boy, restless and happy to be with his dad, climbed on Shah Mohammed's shoulders, and tried to stand there without holding on to the wall. He came sliding down as soon as his mother came into the room carrying trays of food.

There were large plates of rice cooked with lamb, raisins, pistachios, almond, and carrots. Bowls of meatballs, eggplant, pumpkin, *ashak* and *manto* – leek and beef dumplings – and plates of fruits. Everyone gathered around the tablecloth and started eating. Like most Afghans, they ate mostly in silence. Only when they reached the fresh mangoes at the end of the meal did anyone say much.

The wife asked about Corinne and the day's rehearsal.

Shah Mohammed mentioned that someone had asked Corinne before the rehearsal about her children and her husband. "She told us that she had two daughters, but she and their father are divorced."

Shah Mohammed's wife shook her head. "It must be so sad for her not to see her daughters," she said.

"They live with her," Shah Mohammed told her in a tone of astonishment. "It's not like Afghanistan where the children stay with the father until they turn eighteen. And not only that, she told us, 'My former husband and I are still good friends. We just don't live together anymore.'" Shah Mohammed's eyes were wide open as if he could hardly believe what he himself had just said.

"France is a very strange place," his wife observed as she got up to make the tea and bring some of the baklava she had baked earlier that day after returning from teaching her classes at the high school.

It was time to watch one of the Indian soap operas. As his son went to turn on the large flat screen television at the end of the room, Shah Mohammed looked at his children and said to the interpreter, "I would never want to be separated from my children, even for one day."

The Meaning of Love

Kabul. June 2005.

Volleyball is practically the national sport of Afghanistan. Everyone plays it, even if they are not good athletes. The Foundation had a net at one end of the garden. That gave Corinne an idea. One day she suggested to the actors that they play volleyball after they had finished their tea.

Despite the heat, the actors drank their tea with unusual speed and hustled to the net. All the women stood on one side, of course, and all the men on the other. Corinne called out, "Faisal and Shah Mohammed, you change places with Saba and Marina." Everyone laughed; no one moved. Corinne did not push them. One step at a time. She knew she would have to wait a few days.

"Anytime I ask anybody here for anything," she told her friend David one evening, "they say 'It will come to you.' And it does, no matter what I want, or how impossible it seems."

It took a couple of days for some of the women to feel relaxed enough to play on the same side as the men.

Finally, Breshna said to the interpreter, "Tell Corinne that Marina and I will go on the other side, if she gives us ten extra minutes to play." Marina looked startled as Breshna took her hand and pulled her under the net. Nabi and Shah Mohammed took their place on the girls' team.

That was that. Everyone enjoyed it so much that from then on Corinne had a problem getting them to stop playing at the end of the break and return to their rehearsal.

:.:.:.

While the actors whacked the volleyball over the net, Corinne sat under a pomegranate tree with her tea trying to resolve another daunting problem. All the actors had lines packed with emotion, but not one spoke them with any passion. She wondered how Nabi Tanha as Sohrab could show no romantic feelings when he was saying:

> And I, forsooth, in love! I, that have been love's whip;
> Regent of love-rhymes, lord of folded arms,
> The anointed sovereign of sighs and groans,
> Liege of all loiterers and malcontents,
> O my little heart:'
> What, I! I love! I sue! I seek a wife!

Then there was Aref, as Sherzad, who spoke of Maryam:

> O sweet Maryam, empress of my love!
> Vows for thee broke deserve not punishment.
> A woman I forswore; but I will prove,
> Thou being a goddess, I forswore not thee:
> My vow was earthly, thou a heavenly love.

Aref was diffident as he professed his affection, almost cold. And Shah Mohammed as Haroon, King of Kabul, who was meant to be crazy with love when talking about the Princess of Herat, was at best offhand:

> So sweet a kiss the golden sun gives not
> To those fresh morning drops upon the rose,
> As thy eye-beams, when their fresh rays have smote
> The night of dew that on my cheeks down flows.

Why was he not imbuing his lines with the intensity that he brought to his conversations during the tea breaks? Then it hit her. The central element of the play – the idea of "love," at least as Shakespeare meant it – was not making any sense to them.

When she had finally wrested the volleyball from them and got them focused back on the rehearsal, she explained how men and women on her side of the world develop feelings for one another.

"When the four young nobles see the beautiful women from Herat," Corinne said, "they are filled with these feelings. That is what causes them to break their vows." She talked about what it was like to fall in love, but could see she was not being understood, even by Breshna who had described her marriage as a love match.

She knew how much the actors enjoyed sharing deeply held opinions during the breaks, so she decided that day not to continue with a regular rehearsal, but to have a discussion about what love is. She asked all the actors to sit in a circle on the *kilim*, which had migrated to the stage in the garden. By now, the men and the women all sat among each other. That in itself was a big sign of progress.

"This play is called *Love's Labour's Lost*," Corinne said. "If we are going to tell this story, we need to understand what love is." Then she asked each actor to say what 'love' meant to him or her.

"Love has many meanings," Aref said with his usual helpfulness. "I know love best by its spiritual meaning." Like most Afghans, Aref's family had chosen his wife for him. He had not had the same experience as the young nobles in the play. "Love," he said, "is a deep feeling of affection towards something or someone. Those kinds of feelings cause your soul to respond positively to it, and to strongly want it."

"Give me an example," Corinne said.

"For example, I love to pray and do *zikkur* [a Sufi religious ceremony]."

"I entirely agree with Aref jan," Nabi stated. "And I want to add the meaning of physical love. Love is a feeling of intense desire and attraction towards a person. In short, the emotions that lead to sex and romance."

"Sexual passion," Shah Mohammed interjected, serious as always. He still made everyone laugh self-consciously a little.

"That is right," Nabi said. "And also an intense emotional attachment, as well as affection and attraction towards that person."

"Endearment?" Shah Mohammed asked.

"Yes, that is what I mean," Nabi affirmed. He sounded as if he understood what Shakespeare had written about.

Now it was up to Corinne to help him connect the ideas he was expressing to the character he was playing. She also had to get some of the others involved in the discussion. "Let's ask one of the girls," she said.

"I agree with both Aref and Nabi," Breshna Bahar said, "However, I think the meaning of love cannot be explained by words, because our vocabulary is not extensive enough to explain ideas such as love, soul, mind, spirit, essence or conscience. I think that love means an incomparable feeling of affection and solicitude towards someone or something which you have a strong desire to own." Breshna, as many Afghans do, must have had some Greek ancestors. Many ancient statues in Athens have faces with profiles like hers, their serenity frozen in marble forever. As Breshna spoke of love, her usually animated face took on the same calm look.

"What Breshna just said about love, it makes it sound like a selfish word," Leila challenged. "When you love, you have to own it, or else your love will make you suffer. If that is so, then love is a selfish word, and the act of love is a selfish act."

"Then what is love?" Breshna argued sharply. Her calm had vanished in a flash.

"I don't know. I'm still very young. To me love means a feeling of warm personal attachment or strong attraction to another person," Leila responded.

Shah Mohammed intervened again, adding "Something earnest, like affectionate dedication that implies selflessness and abiding feelings."

"Exactly!" Leila exclaimed.

Before Breshna could say anything else – she was making the face she always made when she was getting worked up – Corinne turned to Parwin: "Parwin, you tell us."

"It is simple," Parwin said. "Love means to care, to desire in a respectful manner, to be pleased with and please, to give pleasure and gain pleasure. It can be an intimate sexual relationship between a man and woman. And we use the word 'love' to honor that."

"That is not a complete meaning of love," Faisal challenged. "What you just said is a definition of love from a Western point of view."

"True, true!" everyone exclaimed.

"How so?" Corinne asked. "What is your Eastern definition of love, Faisal jan?"

"Westerners express love along the road," Faisal said, "in bars, at home, on the roof, anywhere, without any regard or respect for it. My definition for love is fondness and devotion of a lifetime for something or someone in a respectful manner."

Nabi joined in. "Everybody knows some sweet lines to say to a girl to attract attention. Real love is in here, in the heart. I've seen Hollywood and Bollywood movies where the guys tell the girls, 'I looked at a flower and thought it was the most beautiful thing I'd ever seen until I met you.'"

Shah Mohammed chimed in sarcastically, "The only place I can meet you is in my dream, and I don't want to wake up."

Dramatically, Breshna added, "I just want you to be happy, even if I'm not the reason for your happiness." Leila made a cheap Bollywood girlish gesture, which made everyone laugh, as she said, "Don't worry, my love, if you fall, I won't let you hit the ground."

Aref looked across the circle at Leila and swooned, "You are my heart, my soul, my treasure, my today, my tomorrow, my forever, my everything!" Everyone roared.

"Oh, yeah, like I would believe that," Leila was fast to reply. They laughed even harder than before.

Faisal adopted a theatrical manner and looked intensely at Breshna. "A candle may melt, and its fire may die, but the love you have given me will always stay as a flame in my heart."

"Shut up, idiot," Breshna hissed, though she was delighted nonetheless with his flirting, even if it was done only in jest.

Parwin wanted to say something, but Nabi interrupted. "My point is," he said, "that these lines don't mean anything. Everybody is capable of reciting such seductive lines all day long. Real love is something rare, and it can't be easily found. Real love is not some kind of a clever line that I can say, or Shakespeare said. Real love is two hearts with one beat. Real love is commitment to a lifetime's devotion, and loyalty at all times until death separates the two.

"In the West, people have built a different concept of love over time. A boy looks at a pretty girl, and falls in love, and vice versa. They fall in love with their appearances. The surface beauty doesn't last very long, however, only to a certain age. What then? Do you spurn your 'beloved' because he or she is not beautiful anymore? And it seems this is exactly what is happening in the West. That is why the rate of divorce is so high, and it is getting higher and higher every year."

Nabi looked at the others and went on, "You may say that is what love means in a civilized country. Then I say that your definition of love and civilization is a monstrous disaster. What about our prophets' times? If your concept of love in the 'civilized' world is expressing your feelings in public, then does it mean that our prophets never experienced love, because they lived in an earlier time, and were not civilized?" He looked at Corinne and continued, "Have you read the story of Prophet Joseph and his master's wife, Zulaikha? It is in the holy books sent by God. Zulaikha fell in love with Joseph's good looks. And we all know the consequences. That is what is happening in your West. That is why the 'falling in love' thing lasts only for a limited time, while in this part of the world, love is true.

"We may not love our wife or husband when we first marry, because it is an arranged marriage. But, over time, it grows into a real love. I'm not saying that every arranged marriage works out for the best. There are many failed ones, but not as many as yours, which you call 'love.'

All the actors were nodding in agreement. Afterwards, Corinne mentioned that the discussion had been one of the most revealing moments yet of her time in Kabul.

"What about you?" Corinne asked the interpreter.

"I agree with everyone," he said, because he was tired from translating all that they had said.

"Even with Parwin?"

"Yes, even with Parwin."

"He agrees even with Parwin," Corinne stated in mock surprise to everyone. She was trying to start a little fight. She liked to do that. It was her way of having fun. In some ways, she was like an Afghan. Then she looked at Marina, "Now, Marina jan, you tell us what you think."

Marina turned crimson and said, "I haven't experienced love yet, and I don't know. Maybe you can ask me this question in ten years."

"OK," Corinne smiled, "I'll remember to ask you this question in ten years." Then Corinne looked at everyone and suggested, "Let's talk about 'hate.'"

The actors exclaimed in one voice, "No!"

"Why?" Corinne asked, surprised at the outpouring.

"Hate is what our country and its people have been cursed with for the past three decades!" Aref said. For once, the smile that had a permanent residency in his eyes was gone.

:::::

From that day, Corinne started to listen more. Sometimes she was still impetuous. And sometimes the actors spluttered in response. But a new feeling had entered the rehearsals.

They were now at the end of the third week, more than halfway to the first performance. Finally, everyone was feeling comfortable with the script. Half of the actors had memorized most of their lines. Sometimes they made mistakes, or added their own words to the text in ways that changed the meanings of whole monologues. Since Corinne did not speak Dari, though, she was unaware of this. She was happy just to hear words coming from their mouths, and their slowly taking ownership of Shakespeare's story.

:::::

In Afghanistan, as in all Muslim countries, Friday – *Jumaa* in Dari, as in Arabic – is the day of rest. Mosques conduct services at midday, attended mostly by men. Extended families gather to have meals together. Rehearsals were never held.

One Friday, Nabi Tanha took his family to the Bagh-e Babur – the garden of the Emperor Babur – for a picnic. His twins and the other children could run around there in one of the few places in Kabul with broad expanses of grass. They rolled down the terraces that had been cut into the slope of the garden's long hill five centuries before. When Nabi was with his family, he made no effort to attract attention. While his kids raced from one tree to the next playing hide-and-seek, he sat quietly with his wife, who was setting out food on a *sofrah*, an eating cloth, laid on the ground. Suddenly he heard a voice he knew well.

"Salaam, Nabi jan." Faisal was standing at a respectful distance, not wanting to invade the privacy of Nabi or his family. "What are you doing here?"

Nabi was glad to see Faisal, but Friday was his day to be with his family. "What are *you* doing here?" he asked back.

"My brothers and sisters are over there under that large acacia tree," Faisal told him. Nabi looked where Faisal was pointing. The gardens were filled with families and he could not make out which one was Faisal's. However, he did see a familiar figure walking up the grand avenue of trees at the center of the garden, trailed by his wife and children. Faisal spotted him too, and waved. Shah Mohammed raised his arm and waved back, then leaving his family briefly on the walkway, he strode towards Faisal and Nabi.

"I didn't know you guys would be here," Shah Mohammed said.

"I think the whole group is here today," Nabi sniffed.

"Maybe we should look for them," Faisal suggested helpfully.

"You can do that," Nabi said. "I want to have some quiet time with my wife and children."

Faisal and Shah Mohammed understood the hint. "*Allah Hafez* [God be with you]," said Faisal. As he and Shah Mohammed turned to walk away, though, Nabi called after them.

"Guys," Nabi hollered. Faisal and Shah Mohammed turned their heads. "Look at the beauty of this place. Maybe we should do a performance here."

"Why not?" Shah Mohammed replied enthusiastically. "That is a wonderful idea."

Faisal's eyes brightened. "We could have everyone in Kabul come to see us!" he exclaimed.

"When Babur was emperor, all the great poets came here to recite for him," Nabi stated.

"Maybe Shakespeare was one of them," Faisal suggested.

"Even if he was not, we can bring him here," Shah Mohammed proposed.

Nabi waved in a way that meant he had nothing more to say. Shah Mohammed and Faisal walked away in separate directions to their families in different corners of the emperor's garden.

Behind the Scenes

Kabul. June 2005.

Mornings for Corinne were a relentless hustle to organize aspects of the production not directly involving the actors.

She needed costumes. Corinne had heard there was an Afghan clothing designer in Kabul who had recently returned from London where for seven years she had managed the women's side of the upmarket British clothing store, Turnbull and Asser. Her name was Shahla Nawabi.

Shahla was born in Kabul but had been forced to flee when she was seven. Her family is related both to the former king of Afghanistan, Zahir Shah, and to the Khan of Qalat, the ruler of the Balouch people, who have no country to call their own but whose lands are spread across Afghanistan, Iran and Pakistan. Those connections had made it dangerous for Shahla's family to stay in Afghanistan after a Communist-led government ousted the king in 1973 and became increasingly repressive. Many of Afghanistan's intellectuals and professionals disappeared without a trace during the years after the coup.

After the Taliban were driven from Afghanistan at the end of 2001, Shahla was among the first Afghans abroad to return home. She had become a successful businesswoman in England and used the skills she had learned there to set up a construction company in Kabul building courthouses and clinics. She was determined to do something useful that women in Afghanistan are not expected to do.

Corinne went to visit Shahla at her home in Shahr-e-Naw where they had tea in a sitting room decorated with sepia-toned photographs of Shahla's notable ancestors.

Shahla immediately understood what Corinne wanted to do with *Love's Labour's Lost*, and agreed to be part of it. The budget for costumes, though, was tiny, just a few hundred dollars. Still, with a bit of imagination, Shahla felt she could come up with something that looked royal and eye-filling. After her many years of designing clothing and jewelry for wealthy women in London, she was excited to be creating something for Afghans.

Shahla suggested that the costumes should draw on the clothes worn by the Turkmen tribes in northern Afghanistan. Turkmen women were less heavily veiled than those from other groups such as the Pashtuns. A stage full of *burqa*-covered women was grimly funny to imagine, but would present a real challenge to the audience. Turkmen women typically wore headscarves over small round caps that vaguely resemble a crown. That would make the girls appear more royal than if their heads were simply draped. Turkmen women also wore elaborate jewelry, and the girls could do the same to emphasize their characters' positions. Better still, Turkmen people were not shy about wearing bright colors, as some other groups in Afghanistan are.

For the boys, Shahla proposed that they wear a simple white *shalwar kameez*, the basic outfits worn by most Afghan males. With some elaborately decorated dark velvet waistcoats, they would look impressive. The velvet was sold at a reasonable cost in the bazaar. The King of Kabul would be given a very fancy turban, and the three others would wear brightly colored round caps. Around their waists, they would tie woven sashes known in Dari, as in English, as cummerbunds.

Shahla made several trips to the large bazaar along the Kabul River in the area known as Mandawi. Though not quite a covered bazaar like the many domed shopping districts in Central Asia, the streets of Mandawi were narrow, and the awnings of the shops covered them from one side to the other, creating the sense of a labyrinth.

One street was lined with vendors selling dried fruit and nuts. Another displayed fighting and singing birds along with hand-crafted cages. Another had walls covered in *burqas* of many colors, lengths and head sizes. Another was stacked with hundreds of the black-and-white cotton headscarves that every Afghan man wears.

Shahla made her way into the heart of the bazaar, where the fabric sellers keep yards of brightly-colored cloth on long rolls. Although Afghan men and women dress in muted tones in public, they fill their homes with lively, sometimes garish, fabrics used for curtains or cushion covers. Much of the brightest fabric of Mandawi ends up as wedding party dresses. For many women, weddings are one of the few occasions when they can go outside their homes. They want to look their best and wear colorful gowns. It was at weddings that they got news of their extended families and looked over prospective brides for their sons.

Shahla understood how Afghan audiences would expect royal women to look. She had seen many productions of Shakespeare in London. *Love's Labour's Lost* was giving her an opportunity to join together two parts of her life.

She asked the cloth salesmen to spread out one bolt of cloth after another. They quickly realized that she was a woman who knew what she was looking for, and responded enthusiastically. She laid one color on top of another to see how each complemented the other. Her goal was to create something that looked richer than the meager budget allowed by selecting colors that worked well together.

She chose a dark velvet for a long skirt for the Princess of Herat and accented it with a green and gold apron, bodice and veil. The Princess's ladies would be in long skirts or *kameez* blouses and baggy *shalwar* pants in shades of dusky rose, mustard yellow and deep fuchsia heading towards violet. The veils, attached to multi-colored Turkmen caps, would come down over the shoulders almost to the knees, and lend a sense of grace, she felt, especially as the girls made their entrances and exits.

Shahla had to settle for imported synthetic fabrics for the most part. She would have loved to use Afghan silk, especially since most of it was produced and woven in Herat, the home of the ladies in this telling of *Love's Labour's Lost*. The silk would have draped more diaphanously, and added a level of grandeur.

All the women's costumes would be heavily embroidered in traditional Turkmen patterns. Ironically the embroidery, which would have been prohibitively expensive in London, cost less in Afghanistan than the cloth itself.

Though the action of the play takes place over several days, Corinne and Shahla agreed to give the ladies only one costume each. They were concerned that audiences unused to theater might have problems following the characters if their appearance changed too often. This was also a way of stretching the limited budget to make the costumes as elegant as possible.

Shahla gathered some seamstresses and got them cutting and stitching.

::::::

Hashmat Ghani Ahmadzai describes himself as the titular leader of the Kuchis, Afghanistan's Pashtun nomads. What better man, then, to ask for a Kuchi tent? One was needed to accommodate the Princess of Herat and her ladies while they were encamped in the King of Kabul's garden.

Kuchi tents are woven from black goat hair and stretched over wooden frames. They provide shelter from the sun during the hottest part of the day, and a place to retire at night. At their best, they are utilitarian. Corinne, however, wanted a tent that was visually stunning. Perhaps Hashmat understood that. From somewhere, he found a white, six-sided tent made of canvas unlike anything a Kuchi would use. It was perfect, though, for *Love's Labour's Lost*. He also contributed some magnificent tent hangings that complemented the Turkmen accent of the costumes.

Hashmat, whose brother, Dr. Ashraf Ghani Ahmadzai, became Afghanistan's president in 2014, always enjoyed sharing his encyclopedic knowledge of Afghan history during meetings about the tent. His trucking business kept many Kuchis employed in the modern equivalent of their ancient tradition as caravan traders. "The Phoenicians controlled the sea routes," he said, "but the Pashtuns controlled the land routes." That was how a Semitic tribe like the Pashtuns found their way into the place that they named the Land of Abram, or Afghanistan, after their great patriarch. But that is a story for another day, and best heard from Hashmat.

⋮⋮⋮⋮

Rahim Walizada was fast emerging as one of the most innovative young carpet producers in Afghanistan. He had lived in New York for ten years, then at the end of the Taliban era came home to Afghanistan and started making carpets with designs unlike any others being woven anywhere. He drew his inspiration from the artist Mark Rothko whose paintings he had seen at New York's Museum of Modern Art. Rothko's large canvases filled with blocks of one or two colors excited Rahim. From the moment he first encountered them, he saw them not as paintings, but as carpets.

Rahim displayed his creations at a shop he had set up at one end of Shahr-e-Naw, away from all the other carpet traders. The foreigners working in Kabul went there in large numbers to buy his unique creations before they were shipped to design centers and high-end carpet shops around the world.

As part of his business, Rahim also gathered many beautiful old rugs from around Afghanistan that he repaired, cleaned and resold. He provided several of these, along with some old woven cushions, to *Love's Labour's Lost*. In the play, they were spread over a bare wooden platform transforming it into a *takht*, a throne, for the King of Kabul and his nobles.

⋮⋮⋮⋮

Props came from wherever they could be found. Musical instruments were borrowed from the Foundation, which had some *tabla* drums and a harmonium, the small two-octave organ pumped by hand that is used in musical performances all over Central and South Asia. The biting rhythms from a well-played *tabla* generate instant excitement. The harmonium, with its mysterious, reedy sound, adds a level of sensuousness and beauty.

A teapot and some Afghan-style cups without handles were borrowed from Corinne's friend David. They were just packed up one day when he was not at home, and no one thought to mention them to him. No one, apart from David, knew that the cups were, in fact, some kind of rare and expensive porcelain. He spent the next few weeks looking everywhere for them.

:::::

And then there was Daoud, the driver. No one behind the scenes was more helpful than Daoud, who became a fixture of *Love's Labour's Lost*. He sat in on many of the rehearsals. He drank tea and played volleyball with the cast on their breaks. He learned most of their lines just from hearing them every day, and could prompt the actors when they faltered, but in a way that made them laugh and not feel self-conscious.

Despite a limited education scratched together in refugee camps in Pakistan, Daoud was able to sort out many problems that were not his obligation to solve. Perhaps it was his ability to laugh in a way that was contagious. Or the joy he took in speaking to everyone, and hearing what was going on in their lives. Perhaps it was his half-dozen gray hairs, which made him look dignified and caused people to ask his advice.

Every day, he picked up Leila and Marina, brought them to the rehearsal, then took them home. On the way home, he often teased Marina, saying things to her like, "Now that you are famous, you must have a line of boys waiting to marry you, all of them good-looking and rich and sophisticated."

Marina always sat in the back where the windows were tinted so that no one walking alongside the car would recognize her. She complained to the interpreter who often rode with them, "If one of my brothers or my father hears him, they will beat him, and they will probably beat me too." Then she giggled.

Daoud loved to sing. He came from a family of well-known singers, and had a sweet voice of his own. Sometimes he sang to Marina. Every day the banter continued until they reached Marina's house, the first stop on the nightly journey home. After Marina got out of the car, Leila would take Daoud to task, saying, "Daoud jan, don't tease her so much."

"All right," he said. They both knew, though, that he would find something else to joke about with Marina the next day. One time, though, after Marina had gotten out of the car, he told Leila and the interpreter very seriously, "She is like my little sister. I would do anything to protect her if anyone even looks at her in a bad or unclean way." They knew he meant it.

After Daoud had dropped off his last passenger, he headed home across the city. He lived in a far corner of Kabul, in an area called Kart-e-Naw. For any other driver, it took an hour to get there. Daoud made the trip in half the time. Singing all the way.

Rehearsals, Act Three

Kabul. August 2005.

One day, Parwin arrived late, shaking. She told the group that she and her husband and their children had been forced to leave their home. "My sister's husband is angry with me because I come home after dark," she said.

When Parwin left the Foundation after rehearsals, she faced a slow ride home. To save money, she took buses instead of taxis. Many times, though, the minibuses that went to her neighborhood sped past her without stopping. Drivers were reluctant to pick up a woman standing by herself. No man would be allowed to share a seat with her, and the driver would lose the fare for that empty seat unless another woman got on. It was even harder for Parwin when she had her kids with her. The drivers were even more unwilling to stop, since they did not charge for children, yet the youngsters each took a space.

With endless waits for two buses and a long way to go, Parwin often did not reach home until nearly 9:00 PM, well after dark. A respectable woman should be in her home by early evening at the latest.

Her sister's husband was an educated man and, at heart, a kind man. Often, though, when he stood outside his gate watering the flowers in front of the wall, or even sometimes when he went to the mosque, his neighbors would mention casually, "I see your sister-in-law comes home after dark." Each time this happened, he smiled politely, but inside he was churning.

"People in the neighborhood are saying bad things behind your back," he told her more than once. "They see you coming home in the night and think you are spending your time with other men."

Parwin knew that her sister's husband understood that she was doing nothing wrong. "I'm working in a Shakespeare play," she would tell him yet again. "How can that be a problem?"

"You and I know who Shakespeare is," her sister's husband would reply, "but the illiterate people in this neighborhood do not." Then one day he added, "They think you're not only an actor, but also a prostitute."

"Let evil fall on anyone who says that!" Parwin exclaimed, horrified. "My husband decides what I should be, and what I can do. He is happy with my work."

"That is what they are saying. I can't live with shame, Parwin jan. I can survive with very little to eat, but not without my honor that I have guarded all my life. Please, you must either quit this play or leave here."

It could not have been a worse time for Parwin and her family to be looking for a place to live. The market for her husband Tawab's business selling imported cars had recently collapsed. He had put all his remaining cash into an auto parts store that had yet to earn a profit.

As Parwin told her story, she also recounted how one day she had been walking home from the bazaar when a man came from behind her on a bike and punched her in the back. "I fell down in the street," she said. "I still have a pain in my leg, because he punched me so viciously. I was with my little son, and I was crying." When she reached home, her husband noticed that she was limping. She told him only that she had slipped on the road; she did not want to worry him.

Parwin also revealed that she had been receiving death threats from the Taliban during the rehearsals, but had not wanted to tell anyone about them.

And now the eviction. She spoke about it in her quiet voice, but it was evident that she was frightened. She explained that she had to leave right away to go with her husband to find a new place to live. She apologized to Corinne and the rest of the cast. Corinne was sympathetic, and thanked her for coming to let her know. She asked if she needed any help from the police. Parwin told her that that would make things worse. She left. She was back, though, the following day, saying only that they had found a place to stay for now, without saying where.

From then on, Parwin brought her son as well as her daughter to nearly every rehearsal, as they had moved too far from his kindergarten. While the actors rehearsed, the youngsters paid close attention to everything that was going on. No matter how many times a scene was repeated, they watched it as if they were seeing it for the first time. Parwin's daughter, Shogufa, was a smiler; her son, Ahmad, was more serious. They were well dressed, and never rolled around on the ground the way most kids do, getting their clothes dirty.

:::::

Love's Labour's Lost was now beginning to take shape, though slowly. The hardest scene for the actors was the third, where the boys and girls are on stage together for the first time. There are a lot of movements. The dialogue must be fast. The focus shifts from one set of characters to another several times. The King of Kabul and the Princess of Herat have to discuss the details of an unpaid loan. It provides the reason why the women have come to Kabul, but beyond this has little to do with what actually happens in the play.

It is a complex scene. The actors had worked on it almost every day since they had started rehearsing, but still it was a mess. Even after the actors began to master their lines, they still did not understand that some of them were supposed to be funny.

One thing that did not make any sense to anybody was that two characters could speak to one another without the others overhearing. Nor did anyone have any sense of the importance of timing in the interplay between the servants acting as messengers between the nobles and ladies.

"No, you are supposed to leave the stage now," Corinne would say as she gently guided an actor out of the way. They would look at the interpreter with unhappy eyes that asked, "Why is she pushing me?" Pushing Afghans is an excellent way to start a fight. He would quickly explain what she was doing. By the time he did, Corinne was already speaking to another actor, and he had to catch up on that conversation.

And then one day, after all the usual interruptions for arguments, urgent trips to the bathroom and tea, they ran the whole scene, and everyone did it perfectly. Corinne clapped vigorously, and the actors applauded themselves. Then they did it again, and it was even better. They had a scene. Characters had come alive. The action was crisp. Lines were spoken as if they were the actors' own words. This was a breakthrough like no other.

Corinne was joyful all the way home, and all that evening as she, David and the interpreter sat up on the terrace of the old fort celebrating a great success. As they ate eggplant sautéed in garlic butter and dribbled with yogurt, they listened to the wind sift through the old acacia tree that arched over the courtyard and the thick stand of lilac bushes at its center. Water gurgled in an eight-sided fountain that David had built.

:::::

The next day when Corinne arrived back at the Foundation, she said, "Let's start by running that scene we all did so well yesterday." The actors took their places.

"OK," Corinne said. "Enter Haroon, Sherzad, Mansour and Sohrab." No one moved. The actors appeared not to remember what they were supposed to do. They looked at one another, and then at their scripts and fumbled through the pages.

Corinne looked as if she wanted to cry, except that she was not a weeper. This time, her voice went up instead of down. "How could you have forgotten everything?" she asked in disbelief.

The interpreter felt sorry for her. And for himself, because this meant he now had to translate all the unhappy things she wanted the actors to hear, and then would have to hear all the unhappy things that the actors did not want him to translate for her. Instead of telling them exactly what Corinne was saying, he simply said to this one and that one, "Don't you remember that when he comes in, you are supposed to go over there and say that?" Then the actors looked at him, and said, "Yes, I remember that. We did that yesterday. Why do we want to do it again?" The interpreter did his best to explain the idea of rehearsing, especially to those who had never done a play before and who were the most puzzled. After a few minutes, the actors found their memories from the day before, and did the scene again, almost perfectly.

Corinne sighed when they had finished and told them, "Let's move on to the next scene."

:.:.:.

The one actor who had the most trouble remembering his lines and his cues was Kabir. He never seemed to know what to do. He was a nice man, and always the first actor to arrive. He did anything that Corinne asked him to do. But he never remembered anything for long. One day, he kept stumbling over lines in scenes he had rehearsed several times. He was supposed to say:

SIKANDER
If my observation, which very seldom lies,
By the heart's still rhetoric disclosed with eyes,
Deceive me not now, the king is infected.

It would come out, though, as "his eyes are infected," or "the king seldom lies." It was all a jumble.

The interpreter took him to one side during the tea break to explain to him that he really needed to try harder to remember things. Very gently he said to him, "Kabir jan, when Corinne tells you to act like a messenger in a scene, you act like a king of old days. When she tells you to act like a funny man, you are too serious.

When she tells you not to move your hands when you talk, you wave them all around. When she tells you to move your hands when you talk, you don't move them. This is a problem. Is there some way to fix it?"

He replied, "I don't know. Sometimes these things happen. They just do. I don't know how to stop them."

He started talking about himself, which he never had before. He said, "During the fighting, I was beaten many times by different factions. Once I was on my way to our house. In our neighborhood, the Uzbeks were in charge. Where I had come from, my brother's house, Gulbuddin [a Pashtun] was in charge. The two factions were fighting each other, sending countless rockets at one another. The Uzbeks thought I was a spy for Gulbuddin. They beat me on the head with the back of their guns, and punched me in the face. Then they kicked me all over my body while I lay crumpled on the floor. I kept shouting that I was not a spy. Still, they kept beating me.

"This same thing happened three or four times with other factions, always for the wrong reasons. I was only trying to take care of my family. As a result, now I can't easily memorize my lines, and I forget my moves. Some may think I'm not a good actor. I used to be," he said as his voice caught. "I used to be a very good actor."

The interpreter told these things to Corinne on the way home that evening. She nodded and looked out through the window at the crowded street. From then on, she treated Kabir more kindly. Slowly, Kabir's confidence started to grow, and he made fewer mistakes. Everyone else helped him as well. After all, he was the oldest person in the group and deserved their respect. And besides, everyone liked him, even though he said little, and rarely told jokes.

:::::

The Afghan and foreign media began coming to do interviews with Corinne and the actors. The actors said good things about the production and how happy they were to be doing the play, and working with Corinne, and experiencing Shakespeare.

Many of the journalists focused on Marina, whom they had seen in *Osama*. They all wanted to hear again how she was discovered by the film's director while she was begging in Kabul. They quoted her as saying, "I had never heard of Shakespeare before this play. Now I like this story from the beginning to the end."

Everyone smiled. But the media attention stirred up an undercurrent of nervousness as the cast suddenly realized the enormity of what they had yet to do.

"This Theater of Heaven"

Kabul. August 2005.

The idea of performing *Love's Labour's Lost* at the Bagh-e Babur came up more and more frequently during tea breaks. Faisal had mentioned Nabi's suggestion to Breshna, who told Leila and Marina, who asked Saba Sahar about it, who then queried Shah Mohammed. When somebody raised it with Nabi, he announced with a wave of his hand, "It was my idea!"

Four performances were already scheduled for the garden of the Foundation. As the production began to take shape, however, thoughts of other, larger venues came up. A number of locations were proposed, but the conversations kept circling back to Babur's garden.

They all knew Babur's story. He was a descendant of Genghis Khan and had come to Kabul in 1504 after being forced out of his homeland in Central Asia. He enjoyed the Kabul valley so much that he stayed there for seventeen years.

"Babur loved the clean air here," Breshna wryly observed one day when the dust and pollution were especially heavy.

"Did he tell you that?" Faisal asked her with an impish grin. She raised her hand as if to swat him.

"He wrote about it in his diary, you potato," she replied. "When you learn to read, you can see this for yourself."

Another day, Shah Mohammed proposed, "We should honor Babur by performing in his garden."

"Who cares about Babur?" Leila said dismissively. "He went off to conquer India and never came back to Kabul."

"Not exactly," countered Saba. "He's buried here."

"If you go to India, Leila jan, and become a Bollywood star," Faisal stated very seriously, "maybe you will have a garden in Kabul named after you as well."

Leila laughed.

Parwin looked at Leila and said, "Leila jan, Shah Mohammed is right. We must respect our history. If we perform at Babur's garden, we will honor our past."

"Isn't the place ruined except for a few trees?" Marina asked. "That is what my father told me. He takes his dogs there to fight."

::::::

Corinne finally had a chance to see the Bagh-e Babur one serene summer evening after a rehearsal at the Foundation. She was curious to have a look at this place that she had heard the actors and others mention. Like them, she had started wondering about additional performances of *Love's Labour's Lost*. When she had broached that thought with David, he had suggested the Bagh-e Babur.

Once the private preserve of the Afghan royal family, Babur's garden had been opened to the public in 1933. For decades after, it had been a favorite destination for Kabuli families seeking a quiet and leafy place, especially on Friday afternoons. Until the fighting ruined it. Recently the garden was being given a new lease on life by the Aga Khan Trust for Culture, which was restoring it as well as several other imperiled historic Islamic structures in Afghanistan.

With Daoud driving, Corinne, David, the interpreter and the American playwright who had helped with the script made their way across the Kabul River on an old German-built bridge. Daoud was softly singing love songs to the women they passed. Below the rim of the closed windows, his hands made gestures of affection. He was steering the car with his knees, nudging it around potholes and past buses with their riders hanging out the doors and off the back, and pushcarts hauled by Hazara laborers who looked too small to move such heavy loads.

The narrow road between the river and a steep mountain was filled with old men in turbans, teenagers in T-shirts, and kids in anything that fit them more or less. Some women wore *burqas*, but most did not. Workers were finishing for the day. The sound of the *azan*, the call to prayer, filled the evening air.

Daoud pulled up at the garden's main gate near the river. Its thick wooden doors rising nearly twenty feet high were shut tight.

"No problem," he chirped in English. He resumed driving alongside the garden's massive, turreted walls, then headed up the mountain to a side gate that was still open near the top of the garden. He swung through it and parked the car in a paved area just below a complex known as the Queen's Palace.

Daoud had visited the Bagh-e Babur a couple of years earlier. It had been bleak and desolate. During the years of civil war, opposing factions had unleashed hundreds of thousands of rockets, many of which had fallen into the garden. The high, thick mud-brick walls that surrounded its near thirty acres had been pulverized in a dozen places, leaving large gaps. Inside, old trees had been cut down by Kabulis desperate for firewood. The fountains had stopped running.

Now, to Daoud's amazement, rows of new trees stretched along each of the cascading terraces that led down to the main gate below. The transformation was astonishing.

Corinne, David and the others were already out of the car admiring the panorama across the Char Deh valley, where a spur of the Hindu Kush mountains in the distance was bathed in evening light. They were soon joined by Jolyon Leslie, a South African-born architect who was leading a team from the Aga Khan Trust for Culture.

Jolyon had trained as an architect at Cambridge University, and had been living in Afghanistan for more than twenty years. He spoke Dari fluently. His name was always noted with respect by foreigners and Afghans alike. With an accent more British than South African, he welcomed the visitors, telling them in his soft-spoken way about the garden and how his organization was restoring it.

David had broached the idea of a performance at the Bagh-e Babur with Jolyon at a dinner in the old fort the week before. Jolyon had immediately voiced approval and invited Corinne to come see whether she could find a spot that would be suitable.

They started by looking at the thirteen terraces that had been sculpted out of the long slope that leads down to the Kabul River. "They almost make natural grandstands," said Jolyon.

"Like an ancient Greek theater," Corinne agreed. "The problem is the trees. They block the view."

"I'm afraid I can't offer to remove them for you," Jolyon replied. "They've all just been planted." Hundreds of men from the rows of squatters' houses that rose up the mountain behind the garden had been hired to plant the trees. Many had been farmers before the fighting had left them homeless; they were happy for the chance to make things grow again. They brought with them the wisdom of generations of Afghan farmers, and made the garden's once-devastated landscape bloom anew. They planted both fast-growing trees to provide some greenery immediately, and others that would one day spread a sheltering crown against the sun as Babur's had.

Jolyon led the way up to a high-walled structure nestled in a corner of the garden at its highest point. It had been built by the king Abdur Rahman in the 1880s for his much-loved third wife, Bibi Halima. It became known as Qasr-e-Malikha, the Queen's Palace.

They entered a tall doorway faced in white marble that was turning pink in the evening light. It led through a long covered arcade.

"We started reconstruction in here only a few weeks ago," Jolyon explained as he gestured everyone to one side as a workman approached them in the passageway hauling out two buckets of rubble.

The arcade opened onto a terrace that stretched a hundred feet, connecting the two wings of the palace. Along the back of the terrace where the heart of the old palace had stood, only five towering arches remained. Below the terrace and stretching between the wings was a large courtyard enclosed on the fourth side by a high wall pierced with arched openings. The courtyard, large enough to hold three or four tennis courts, was a very private place wrapped in sweeping views. It was easy to imagine long-ago summer evenings like this one, with breezes carrying the scent of roses from the acres of garden beyond.

Building materials and wooden planks were scattered in piles across the terrace, as well as in the courtyard. Still, the space had a regal quality about it. Jolyon led the group down one of two curving flights of eighteen stone stairs that flowed from the terrace to the courtyard. The terrace itself was fronted by a row of five half-round buttresses built with chiseled stone blocks. They looked like the battlements of a castle.

"Those arches must have created a very grand living space," Corinne mused.

"They did," Jolyon agreed. "In later times, the palace was used as a royal guest house when the king received delegations from abroad."

"If the terrace weren't quite so high above the courtyard, it would almost be a natural stage," Corinne said.

Gesturing toward the arches, David added, "You could not design a more dramatic set for a million dollars."

The two wings at either end of the terrace had managed to remain partially intact. Jolyon suggested they take a look at the one on the far side from the entry. It had not suffered as much damage as the other parts of the building. Inside it was a marble-tiled *hamam* – a steam bath – whose decorative plaster had somehow remained unscathed by the ravages of time, war and neglect. It was a small gem of a room. Very little imagination was needed to conjure the ladies of the court lolling on the warm stones, as the soothing heat made them feel fresh.

"I want to come here every night after rehearsals," Corinne fantasized. "Jolyon, can you have somebody prepare it for me?" Jolyon smiled, but said nothing.

::::::

Corinne began thinking aloud as she visualized how the play might be presented amid the ruins. She moved back and forth across the terrace, then behind the five high arches, then down the sweeping staircases to the courtyard, and then back up again.

She asked questions. Jolyon proposed solutions. New questions. More ideas, which were flying and then discarded and replaced like kites in the evening wind. Everyone offered thoughts of their own. The decisions, it was clear, however, would be made by Corinne.

There were problems. The terrace really was too high to be used as a stage. Better to set up a low stage in the courtyard below in front of the terrace's battlements. But the remains of a ruined fountain sat just where the performance should be. Jolyon insisted that the fountain could be removed, the hole filled and the rough terrain around it could be smoothed. That was hard to visualize.

Someone proposed that the girls make their initial entrance riding camels. It would be very dramatic if they entered from a gatehouse in the lower corner of the courtyard that had allowed the queen's curtain-draped carriage to be driven into it with all her retinue unseen. The camels could be brilliantly decorated with canopied seats, elaborate weavings and tassels and bells.

For the next several weeks, the search was on to find camels. Daoud was dispatched to the large livestock market at Kampani to look for camel drivers who might understand what was needed. He talked to some Kuchi nomads he saw passing through Kabul with a mother camel and her newborn. He even checked with the Kabul zoo, but all to no avail. In the end, the idea of the camels was dropped. It was decided that if one of them were to panic and charge the audience, the results would have been dramatic in a way no one wanted.

Finally, Corinne made her decision. If Jolyon was absolutely sure he could get rid of the fountain – he was – and could smooth out the earth in the courtyard – he could – then Corinne would have the actors perform on the courtyard level with the battlements as their backdrop. Indeed, the battlements made the space in front of them truly look like the walls of the castle of a king.

The palace and its courtyard that had once been filled with flowers were a love poem that Abdur Rahman had written for his favorite queen. Only a king could compose on a scale like this. The labors of his love may have been scarred by time, but they had not been lost. And they would be used to the fullest.

::::::

Jolyon led the way out of the Queen's Palace enclosure through the carriage-high arches of the royal gatehouse. They stopped for a few minutes to look at the pieces of carved marble grave markers temporarily stored there. Translators were working through the inscriptions on them, trying to reassemble the fragments into the complete stones they once had been. Most had been shattered by the rockets.

With the sun now sinking behind the tips of the mountains, they strolled along the top of Babur's garden from where they could see a caravanserai-like structure that Jolyon's team was building just inside the main gate at the bottom of the slope below.

"A real caravanserai stood there in centuries past," he told them. Indeed, the narrow street between the gate and the river where Daoud had driven them was one of the many strands of the fabled network known as the Silk Road.

They kept walking until they reached a small mosque constructed by Shah Jahan to honor his ancestor Babur. Miraculously, it had not been destroyed in the fighting. Its marble walls had been delicately carved along their edges into crescents of stone lace. Six elaborate finials crowned its flat roof. Its design had clearly come from the same minds that had created the Taj Mahal, which Shah Jahan also had built.

"Mughal emperors came from India several times to this garden to pay homage to Babur," Jolyon told them. He showed them the inscription that Shah Jahan had ordered to be placed in the mosque. In part it reads:

> ... only this mosque of beauty, this temple of nobility, constructed for the prayer of saints and the epiphany of cherubs, was fit to stand in so venerable a sanctuary as this highway of archangels, this theater of heaven, the light garden of the God-forgiven angel king whose rest is in the garden of heaven, Zahir-uddin Muhammad Babur the Conqueror.

"This theater of heaven." That seemed a good omen.

Exits and Entrances

Kabul. August 2005.

One day during the fourth week of rehearsals, after yet another dispute with Corinne about some small thing, Nabi Tanha announced to the interpreter that he did not want to play his part unless he received more pay than the other actors. "I have more lines and movements than everyone else," he announced, "and I should be paid more than the others." He stood in the center of the stage in the Foundation's garden.

"Everyone gets paid the same amount, no matter how many lines they have," Corinne told him.

"If you want me to play my part," Nabi said. "I have to bring some changes into the text, and into all our movements. I'll show you how to do it. Or at least you have to ask me for my help."

"Is this some kind of a joke?" Corinne asked. "I'm the director, not you."

Nabi ignored her. "Everyone everywhere respects me, but you don't think of me even as a walnut." He was working himself up to a big scene. His back was straight. He stood as if he were giving orders. "Nothing is more important in the world to me than respect," he went on. "If someone respects me, then that is everything for me. Here you look at me as you see the others. I'm different from the others. My education, my acting, my personality, my sense of humor, my knowledge of the theater and so on. You have to acknowledge all these, otherwise I'll leave this project. If you still treat me like the others, and pay me only as much as the others, then you have to swap my part with someone else's and give me a smaller one."

The interpreter took a deep breath and started translating all this to Corinne, who then began speaking forcefully to Nabi.

"I do respect you, but you're no different from the others. We're all the same. I know you're more educated than the others, but your education isn't special. If you want me to change your part, I can do that. But you must learn it and stay with it from now on. You have to stand by your word. You were the one who said, 'If you were with us for six months, we could challenge the whole country.' Now you want to challenge me. You want to be the director. You want to change the text. You want to do things that aren't yours to do. But you're afraid of having so many lines. So, how would you do all these other things?"

Nabi drew himself up and spoke quietly, with anger burning in his eyes. "Yes, you're absolutely right," he said, "and I am absolutely wrong! Now I am leaving. You can cast someone else instead of me. Good luck! Goodbye!"

Corinne looked at him with her mouth open. "What?"

"I said I am leaving," Nabi repeated. "I don't want to be part of this project anymore."

"OK. No problem," Corinne replied.

"Once again," said Nabi who was milking the moment, "goodbye, and I shall never see you again." He started to walk off the stage, and toward the door.

Saba came over to Corinne and spoke to her quietly for a moment, saying she needed to go out for a few minutes. Corinne nodded distractedly. Saba followed Nabi out of the door. All the other actors started chattering to one another. Corinne busied herself with the text. Every couple of minutes, she asked someone about something they did not need to talk about. She seemed a bit lost.

Nabi and Saba came back. Nabi pointed at Corinne and said, "I was leaving, but Saba didn't let me. She said it is rude to leave like this. I came back only because of her, not you."

Corinne looked at him like he was someone she found annoying.

"Then work for Saba," she said. "Not for me. You're not part of my project anymore. I don't need you."

Nabi was now defiant. "No! I'm going be in this play, and work for you, and you have to change my part."

"Are you instructing me," Corinne asked in disbelief, "or making a suggestion to me?"

Nabi turned stoic. "Whatever you think."

Perhaps Corinne's father had taught her the ways of the bazaar at an early age, or maybe they were just in her blood. She knew the art of bargaining better than most, as she had demonstrated in the carpet stores in Kabul. She could haggle over the prices like an Afghan. She knew all the tricks. Her mind seemed to be moving in that direction now. She was looking to make a deal. "I'll swap your part with Aref's," she said.

"That would be difficult for me," Aref interjected, politely. "I've already memorized all my lines, and I have my exams at the university soon. I don't have time to memorize someone else's lines. We had to decide these things four weeks ago, not now. I'm sorry, Nabi jan, you have to find another way to solve your problem, not me."

Aref was not part of Nabi's faction. Nabi could not tell him what to do. He dismissed Aref with a wave of his hand and said, "Fine. I am leaving. This is the last time I say this." Then he pointed at the other actors and said, "I warn you people, you won't achieve anything by doing this stupid project. You have to listen to me, otherwise you will regret this one day. You have to understand that this play will have repercussions. You will all become targets. It'll become a threat to your life and your family. Goodbye!" Nabi picked up his bag and started to leave.

The interpreter did not want to translate.

"I thought you were coming back," Corinne said. "What is happening?" By then, Nabi was out of the door. "Is he coming back?" she asked.

"No," the interpreter said.

Corinne shook her head and looked at the actors, who were all quiet. "Aref," she said, "you have to play Nabi's part. I'll find someone else for your part."

The first performance was in less than two weeks.

∴∵∴

The next several days were difficult as rehearsals continued without Nabi. By the end of that week, only about two-thirds of the play had been blocked out. The actors were remembering most of their lines and movements, but Aref had to read Nabi's part from the script, while the interpreter read his. Then Corinne started catching many kinds of sickness. The weather was getting even hotter, some days reaching 110°F. The actors started arriving late again, and becoming impatient and smoking cigarettes in the middle of rehearsals. Every day, someone had diarrhea. The costumes were not ready, though the seamstresses were working hard. Not all the props had been sourced as yet. Someone always seemed to have something discouraging to say. Several cast members began to feel that the play was not going to happen and whispered their thoughts to the others.

Corinne, who was visibly ill, lost her temper when Parwin was having trouble remembering everything she was supposed to do. Crestfallen, Parwin told Corinne quietly, but insistently, "You have to understand me, Corinne. How many things should I do at once? I am thinking of what should I cook for tonight. Acting here, listening to your explanations, understanding my lines, keeping my eyes on my daughter and son who are wandering in the garden there, thinking that they may hurt themselves. And I have no idea whether my husband is still at work or if he will come home late tonight. Do we have electricity tonight? If we don't, how can we sleep without a fan? We have so many mosquitoes. I don't know why people don't have eyes to see me and understand me."

∴∵∴

146

Every day, Shah Mohammed went looking for Nabi after the rehearsal to try to convince him to rejoin the play. One day, he found him in his cramped studio in Shahr-e-Naw at the back end of a video shop. He told Nabi everything that was happening at the Foundation with Corinne and the other actors. Nabi brushed him off.

"Look at all the projects I have," Nabi said, pointing to a pile of papers on his desk. "The Germans want me to make a film for their training center. I have to make three new commercials for these Afghan companies selling ice cream. How do I have time for stupid things like Shakespeare?"

Another day, when Nabi was not in his studio, Shah Mohammed tracked him down at his house and told him everything again as they sipped tea in Nabi's living room. The day after that, he found Nabi at the Afghan National Television office. On the next day, when Shah Mohammed again asked Nabi to stop being stubborn and rejoin the group, Nabi said, "What do I have to say to make you understand that I'm done with Corinne and her play?"

Nabi had always listened to Shah Mohammed before. So why not now? It was only while he was shaving the next morning that Shah Mohammed suddenly understood the problem. Nabi was a morning person. In the evening, when he was tired, he became grumpy and would say "No" to any suggestion. Shah Mohammed carefully formulated a plan.

On Friday morning, he woke up early and took a taxi to Nabi's house. He knocked on the door and waited. There was no answer. He knocked again. After he had waited for five more minutes and no one had opened the gate, he turned around to go home, feeling deflated. He thought Nabi and his family must have gone early to some picnic site, which they often did on the weekends. Then he saw Nabi standing across the road with a bundle of warm *naan* and a cage of eggs, looking at him.

"What are you doing here so early?" Nabi asked.

"Do you have petrol in your motorcycle?" Shah Mohammed asked.

"Yes."

"I want to take you somewhere."

"Now?"

"Yes."

"Where?"

"Just come."

"I want to have my breakfast first. Why don't you join us? Last night my wife made some baklava."

Shah Mohammed's stomach growled with hunger. He looked at the twenty eggs carefully set in the birdcage Nabi used for carrying them. He decided not to go inside. Nabi would pry from him why he was there and disrupt his plan. He made himself sound serious. "I haven't had breakfast either," he said. "Get your motorcycle, please."

"At least let me give the *naan* and eggs to my wife."

:::::

Shah Mohammed mounted the motorcycle and instructed Nabi to sit behind him. That had never happened before. Shah Mohammed sped through Kabul's streets, which were empty of traffic on a Friday morning. After half an hour, they reached the side gate of the Bagh-e Babur. It was closed. Shah Mohammed knocked a couple of times. Slowly the large wooden gate eased inward on its hinges.

"We don't open until nine o'clock," a doorman with a walkie-talkie explained through the partially opened door. "Come back in two hours." Then the man noticed Nabi, recognizing him immediately. "Oh! For Mr. Bulbul, this garden is open twenty-four hours a day." He pulled the door wide and graciously invited Nabi to come in. Shah Mohammed thanked the doorman and drove through the gate.

"Are you going to tell me why we are here?" Nabi asked unenthusiastically as he got off the motorcycle. "I was planning to come later with my family."

Shah Mohammed did not answer. He parked the motorcycle and walked across the garden to the place where Babur is buried. Nabi watched him go, then followed.

As he stood in front of Babur's grave, Shah Mohammed held his hands open in front of him and recited a short prayer. Nabi watched but did not join in. When he had finished, he began to speak to Nabi as if he were instructing a pupil. "Babur was once a powerful emperor," he said. "When his oldest son was dying from a strange illness, Babur made a deal with Allah. He prayed, 'Let my son live, and you can have my life.' Babur was only forty-seven years old. Soon after, he died. His son lived, and the Mughal dynasty lasted for more than two hundred years."

"Are you giving me a history lesson now, or playing some kind of a prank?"

Shah Mohammed pointed to the inscription on Babur's grave. "Can you please read that for me?"

"I thought you had something important for me," Nabi said with annoyance. "Fridays are my family time. I'm going home."

"Then let me read it for you," Shah Mohammed said. "'If there is a paradise on earth, it is this, it is this, it is this.'"

Nabi turned and walked out of the grave enclosure. Shah Mohammed said to him in a louder voice, "Nabi jan, Babur felt he was in Paradise when he was in Kabul."

"So?"

"Sometimes you have to make a deal to make things better. Babur made a deal with Allah. The price was high, but he got what he wanted. How high is your price? What will make you come back to the group you yourself put together? Are you so selfish that you will walk away from your friends and colleagues? We all respect you. Don't you have a shred of respect for us?"

Nabi stopped, but did not answer.

"Are you not the one who first suggested we should do a performance here? Do you not remember that Friday when you said that to Faisal and me? It was only a few weeks ago. Now it has been arranged. But you have abandoned us. Why? Because of Corinne?

People like her come and go, and yet we Afghans always stay together. We have faced the Russians, the British, the Pakistanis, and now the Americans. None of them has ever listened to what we say. They don't care who we are. They don't know our history or respect our culture. We have held hands and stuck with one another. That is why we still exist as a country. We don't leave each other." Shah Mohammed had caught Nabi's attention. Nabi stared at him, but remained silent.

Shah Mohammed walked out of the grave enclosure onto the grass. He spread his arms wide and shouted, "If there is a paradise on earth, it is this, it is this, it is this."

Nabi stood there silently for a minute, then he burst out laughing and hurried back to the gate. By the time Shah Mohammed had caught up with him, Nabi was gone with his motorcycle. Shah Mohammed shrugged. He had tried. He thanked the doorman as he went out to the street to find a taxi.

:::::

Nabi came back to rehearsals the next day while the actors were in the middle of running a scene. Everyone stopped as he entered the garden. Corinne looked at him with surprise and asked sarcastically, "Have you come to watch us?"

Nabi was unusually subdued. "No, no!" he said with surprise in his voice, "I have come back to join the play."

"That's interesting," Corinne said in a voice that made it clear that she did not find it interesting. However, she had not been able to find an actor in the week that Nabi had been gone. Her bazaar haggling instincts swung into action. She said nothing else, and waited for Nabi to make the next move.

Nabi put down his bag at the edge of the stage as he climbed the three steps to join the others. "I needed the time to reflect," he said, staring at Corinne. "Now I regret my past actions. I should not have behaved that way." Then he looked at everyone else in the room, "I thought a lot about all of you this week," he went on. "Finally,

I found myself guilty. I tried hard not to come back, but my conscience wouldn't let me stay away any longer. In fact, my heart takes me everywhere, not my feet." Then he looked at Corinne. "I dreamt several times about our fighting," he said. "I saw both of us in my dream. I found myself stupid and foolish."

His usual lofty demeanor was nowhere to be seen that day. "I know I was wrong," he went on. "Now I want to be part of this play. Or if you don't give me my part back, I'll play any part you want me to. If you don't want me to be a member of this project, I'll stay here until you give up and give me a part to play. I don't care about my salary. Just show some respect. That is all. Not just towards me, but to everyone else. That is all."

"I don't want to talk about the past," Corinne stated calmly. "If you want to be a member of this project, you have to play Aref's part."

Nabi brightened immediately. "That is great," he said. "I really appreciate it. I'll do my best to bring happiness to you."

Saba gave Nabi one of her arch looks, and said teasingly, "I would be surprised if you mean that."

"You shouldn't put yourself in the middle of this," he snorted back. "It is none of your business."

"What about us?" Parwin spoke. "Are we none of your business, too?"

"Please don't start again," Nabi pleaded. "I just talked for all of you. The respect part. You also have to know that I have emotional problems sometimes. My brain doesn't work sometimes. It is all the result of the war. Then I think about my stupidity, and suffer for weeks. I don't want to talk about anything I did. Let me concentrate on my lines. I have a lot of work to do."

The rest of that day was good. Everyone worked hard. Nabi made many jokes. He also told everyone to concentrate on their movements and lines to keep Corinne happy. Suddenly, scenes that had always been a shambles started to flow. Aref had already learned most of his new lines in the week Nabi was away. That was a challenge for Nabi to learn all of his new lines as fast as possible.

Ironically, with Nabi's change of roles in *Love's Labour's Lost,* he and Breshna were once again paired up.

:::::

The day after Nabi returned, a phone started to ring in the middle of rehearsal, even though Corinne had clearly instructed everyone to turn off their mobiles. It sounded extra loud because they were working inside that day.

"Whose phone is that?" Corinne asked sharply.

Breshna had run to her large bag at the side of the room and was milling through it looking for the ringing phone. "Sorry," she said. "I have to answer it."

"No! We're not going to stop while you take a call," Corinne insisted. "I myself turned off my phone. How many times has it been said that we turn off our phones during rehearsal? You know the rule!"

Having located her mobile, however, Breshna was raising it to her ear. "This will take only a moment," she said in English, "then I'll respect the rule."

"No! No! You'll respect the rule right now, this minute!" The anxieties of the past weeks and the looming date of the first performances all jumped into Corinne's face; she looked angrier than anyone in the cast had ever seen her.

"Shut up, you fool!" Breshna shouted at her in Dari. "You and your rules! Your rule is not God's rule! I can break it. This is my boss at the Ministry of the Interior. I must take his call." By then the call had cut itself off. She walked away saying, "Now I have to call him back."

The interpreter knew he should not translate anything.

Everyone was looking at Breshna as she punched in the number. She narrowed her eyes as she spoke with her boss. Her face became inflamed and red.

"When did it happen?" Breshna shouted into the phone, "Where? Give me the address! Who's involved? Did you recognize any of them? Were they Pakistanis? How much were they carrying?"

No one knew what she was talking about.

Corinne was all worked up by then. She did not need a side-show by Breshna on top of everything else. "Enough! Enough!" she stated in her deepest and most authoritative voice. "We can't wait for you. Let's start."

Breshna was throwing her phone back into her bag, and she was even more agitated than Corinne. "Do you know what happened?" Breshna yelled in Dari. "Of course not! You just stand there, yelling 'Enough! Enough!' while a gang of Pakistani criminals is trying to smuggle hashish and heroin from Afghanistan to Pakistan. It is my job to arrest them." Then she added in English, "I have to go."

"Absolutely not!" Corinne stated indignantly, not having understood the rest. "You can't just leave in the middle of rehearsal. You were already late coming today. You don't know your lines, your movements and …"

Breshna looked at Corinne as if she were totally insignificant. "Yes, I can leave now," she said. "I don't care for your rehearsal, your lines, your movements …" she fumed as she zipped her bag. "I can't stay here and let a bunch of stupid Pakistanis corrupt my country. Enough! We are sick of these criminals in Afghanistan. We have to stop them, and that is my job. See you tomorrow. Goodbye!" She ran out of the door, and was gone.

Corinne looked at everyone with disbelief. Chattering broke out among the actors.

One said, "Breshna did what she had to do."

Another said, "I think she was right."

The next said, "She could have done it tomorrow."

A fourth said, "How could she do that tomorrow? Let them go to Pakistan and arrest them there?"

Corinne just walked slowly out of the room, and no one saw her for an hour. Though it was early, the actors decided to go and have their tea. And, of course, since Breshna was not there, they all talked about her.

Corinne was not sure whether to be angry with Breshna or to sympathize with her. She got up to have a cup of tea and worked the rest of the afternoon with the actors who were still having problems with their lines.

∷∷∷

Breshna came back two days later. Corinne did not say anything to her. In the world of professional theater, Breshna would have been fired. Corinne knew, though, that she could not find anyone to replace her in the short time before the show opened. There was little more than a week left until the first performance. And at this point, the actors had yet to rehearse the whole play.

Things, though, were moving faster every day. The actors had finally begun to get a sense of what it was like to be on stage. They were catching on to basic stage tricks, like how to speak to each other while also speaking to the audience. The women were forgetting to be shy with the men. Now they were looking into each other's eyes when they spoke and standing next to the men when they needed to. The good feelings had come back again, but one of the most difficult scenes lay ahead.

Expulsion of the Russians

Kabul. August 2005.

The tea break was over. The volleyball had been put away. Corinne gathered the actors on the stage at the end of the garden and had them sit along its edge. She had been very sick that morning and she was still not feeling well. She was determined, though, to block the next scene before she quit for the day.

"Today we have reached what is probably the funniest scene in the play" she told them. "By now, as you know, the four nobles have confessed to each other that they are in love with the women and want to go to see them. They are ashamed, however, to tell the women that they have decided to break their vow of celibacy. So, they come up with the silly idea that if they disguise themselves, the women will not recognize them. They dress up as Russians."

The actors looked at each other with sour expressions. Faisal, wanting to be sure he understood her correctly, asked, "Russians?"

"Yes," she replied, and asked them to start reading the scene from the script. No one did. Shah Mohammed had the first line, spoken to Marina:

HAROON
Will you not dance?

He looked at the script. He looked at the others. He said nothing.

Nabi Tanha, despite everything that had happened, still saw himself as the spokesman for the others. He looked at Corinne with disbelief in his eyes. "Japan won its independence one day before us," he said gravely. "Look where they are today, and where we are now. We are so backward. We live in the thirteenth century. Why? Because of politics. Who is responsible for our backwardness? England and Russia. The permanent wounds that the Russians left behind, in our hearts and in our souls, they're still fresh. Corinne, now you put salt on fresh wounds by telling us to disguise ourselves as Russians. How can you do this to us?"

Corinne was taken aback. She did not know what to say. She looked around at the other men.

"I do not think we should be Russians," Shah Mohammed added quietly.

Faisal quickly agreed. "He's right," he said. "It is a disgrace to us, to our nation, and our history."

"We cannot be Russians," said Aref.

The girls were nodding as well.

Somehow in the lengthy reading of the script in the first week, none of them had understood that the boys were meant to be Russians. Everyone had ignored the stage direction in italics, thinking it was for the director, not themselves.

It was near the end of the day. Corinne did not have the energy to discuss it with them. She looked at the interpreter and just shook her head slowly as she did when she was beyond her wits' end.

The interpreter stepped in and asked the actors for possible solutions. They had a hard time thinking of anything other than that under no circumstances were they going to be Russians.

"What about Indians?" the interpreter asked in English, just trying to think of something. Corinne did not say "No," as she usually did to suggestions. She decided to go home, and left looking discouraged, without saying goodbye. She did not even call from the car, which she had always done on the other days when she had left early.

⸛⸛⸛⸛⸛

The interpreter suggested that they all sit in a circle. Now the actors had to come up with something. He took out a notebook and pen, and asked each of them if they had any ideas how to make the scene about Indians instead of Russians. He had never talked to them in this way. It was not his position to tell them what to do, since he was younger than all of them except for Marina and Leila.

One actor proposed including an Indian song, another suggested doing some Bollywood dancing. Maybe they could wear Gandhi-like clothes or Indian turbans or the Hindu red dot on the forehead. Another thought they should wear Indian royal slippers.

"These are all interesting ideas," the interpreter noted, "but we need to work these things into the script." The actors nodded in agreement. No one said anything.

"Let's do an improvisation," he suggested. "Let me invite a few Afghans who work here at the Foundation to watch." He knew the actors loved performing in front of an audience. If it were up to him, he would have invited in a bunch of people from the street every day to see what they were doing. That way, they would have worked harder.

Ten minutes later a small audience had been gathered. The interpreter gave each of them a pen and paper, and asked them to jot down their reactions to the scene that was about to be improvised.

The actors began. They each sang a Bollywood song and danced. They were hilarious, but they did not know what to say when they had finished singing. One of them told a joke in Urdu that made everyone laugh. Nearly everyone in Afghanistan understands Urdu from watching hundreds of Bollywood movies every year. Indeed, many Afghans speak Urdu well, especially those who lived in Pakistan as refugees.

This gave the interpreter an idea. He collected the papers from the audience. Some had written only one line, while others had filled the whole page, back and front. The actors went home for the day and the interpreter promised them a script by the next afternoon. He asked them to come one hour early to work on what he planned to write overnight, translating the Dari of the Russian scene into Urdu.

When he reached home, his five sisters, brother and parents were sitting around a tablecloth in the living room, having their dinner. His mother went to the kitchen and brought a plate of rice with meatballs, and put it in front of him. She asked him about his day. He told them about the actors refusing to do the Russian scene. His parents said they agreed with the actors. After the interpreter had finished his dinner, he went to his room, while his family remained in the living room to watch the popular Indian soap opera, *Tulsi*.

The interpreter had never thought about writing a play before. But why not? Now he had his chance. He worked late, writing jokes, discarding them, writing more, until he had a scene – in Urdu. All the time, he kept referring back to Shakespeare's lines to make sure he did not change things too much.

When he had finished the ten pages, it was past midnight. He went to the living room, and found his mother half asleep in front of the TV. His father, sisters and brother had gone to bed in their rooms and were sound asleep. He turned off the TV, and gave his mother what he had written. He asked her to read it. First she begged off, saying that she was tired and that she had to brush her teeth and go to bed. When the interpreter insisted, she put on her glasses, yawned and started reading. After glancing at the first line, she looked at him and said, "It's in Urdu."

"Yes, I know it is," he replied.

She went on reading.

"Is this part of somebody's play that you copied?" she asked him.

"No, I wrote it myself to replace Shakespeare's Russian scene."

She began reading the lines out loud. Then she started to laugh. The more she read, the harder she laughed. Each time she tilted her head back to laugh, he felt a wave of satisfaction sweep over him. He wondered what would the actors think. And more importantly, what would Corinne say.

⁙⁙

The next afternoon, the actors all showed up early, as requested. Corinne was not yet at the Foundation. The interpreter led the actors in some vocal exercises the way Corinne always did, then gave the boys the script, and walked them through it a couple of times.

They all laughed, and liked it. They made a few changes until everyone was happy with their lines. When Corinne came, the interpreter said to her, "The actors want to do some Indian improvisations we created to replace the Russian scene last night."

"No," she said. She was worried that the days were passing and they were making little progress. That day, however, the actors would not accept "No." They told her very politely that they were going to do the scene, and took their positions.

"Go ahead, then," Corinne said since she saw that she could do nothing to change their minds. "Quickly, because we don't have much time to waste." She slumped onto a chair, still drained by her sickness from the day before.

The actors began. Nabi was the first to come on stage and sing. The interpreter looked at Corinne to observe her reaction as Nabi wiggled his way into position. As soon as he started, she sat up. Her exhaustion eased from her face as she chuckled, then laughed out loud, even though she had no idea what the actors were saying. She could not stop. Nor could the girls.

The sound of everyone's laughter brought the employees of the Foundation, who were curious to see what was going on. The actors were energized by having the audience, which kept on growing as more employees arrived. The audience hooted raucously. When the scene was finished, they demanded to see it again. The actors did it a second time, and everyone laughed even more than before.

"Great job!" Corinne said, "We don't need to work on this scene again. Let's focus on some others."

"I'm on the same level as Shakespeare," the interpreter bragged.

"Don't let it go to your head," Corinne chided him with a smile.

"Well, you laughed harder at my jokes than you did at Shakespeare's," he pointed out to her. "I'm just saying."

"You're cheeky!" Corinne said and made a face at him. He did not mind. That meant she was feeling better.

:·:·:·:

Later that day, they did the Indian scene again. The interpreter had called Qaseem Elmi, and invited him to come watch the rehearsal and catch any errors in the Urdu. Qaseem spoke Urdu fluently.

Qaseem had never seen a play before, and was transfixed by the level of intensity that came from having actors perform in front of him. He was accustomed to hearing actors speak from a screen. He was amazed to see that the script, on which he had worked so hard, was in fact filled with so much life.

Everyone on the Foundation staff who had seen the actors' earlier performance had told the other workers about it. When they heard Nabi begin his song again, they all rushed out of their offices and into the garden. Their laughter swiftly became a roar.

Daoud was clapping in time to the music, as were many others. Qaseem was holding his hands wide apart in the air and moving his shoulders as if he were dancing Punjabi *bhangra* style.

:·:·:·:

That same day the costumes arrived. They were so beautiful; just looking at them excited everyone. Shahla Nawabi brought one of her seamstresses with her and made a few adjustments to the girls' dresses. Everything fit well and the costumes made them all look royal. The interpreter went out to buy a large watermelon for every one to celebrate.

:·:·:·:

Two days later, though they had hardly finished blocking the final scene, the cast held a dress rehearsal. The stage at the end of the garden had been removed overnight to make room for the chairs for the audience. The actors would be performing on the grass in the centre of the garden, on the same spot where Corinne and the actors had sat five months before on the Hazaragi *kilim* and talked about doing a play.

For a first full run-through, it was not bad. Corinne, though, was not happy with it. Some of the actors forgot to come on stage when they were supposed to. Others twisted their lines in a few places. By now the interpreter had heard the lines so often that he could correct them without consulting the script. Corinne sat back and watched.

The next afternoon, the actors went first to the salon, sat in a large circle and read through the script together. Afterwards, they did another run-through in the garden. It was one of those days when no one seemed to remember what to do. There were long waits for actors who had forgotten to make their entrances. Props could not be found.

The first performance was in two days. The truth was that the actors were not ready, but what could they do? The Foundation had already sent out invitation cards.

Performance

Kabul. 31 August 2005.

Opening night. Corinne was anxious and did not know what to expect. For the first time, all of the actors arrived at the Foundation on time. They all used one dressing room and put on their costumes quietly. The men went in first, and when they were finished, the women used it. They had come a long way from the days when the girls would not look at the boys. They had decided themselves that they all wanted to be together in one room. No one wasted time chatting, or using the bathroom, or drinking tea, or eating, or smoking, or arguing about unimportant issues. Everyone had a script in hand and was going over their lines. They all looked nervous.

The garden of the Foundation filled up as soon as the doors opened. Foreigners were offered the seats in the first row. Afghans filled the other seats, all talking to one another. About a hundred chairs had been set out in a semi-circle around the playing area. Within minutes, they were filled.

Mustafa Haidari, who worked at the Foundation, was the one who always solved everyone's problems. Anything that anyone needed, Mustafa would make it appear or happen. Now he was racing around with other Foundation staff locating additional chairs as people continued to pour in. Corinne watched everything from behind a window facing the courtyard. With all the seats filled, some of the later arrivals settled on the carpets in the playing area, not understanding that this was where the actors would be appearing shortly. One man tried to set a chair between the *takht* of the King of Kabul and the tent of the Princess of Herat. Mustafa was there to redirect him.

The ever-increasing audience was the kind of problem that any theater impresario anywhere could only dream about. In the end, no one ever really knew how many were in the audience. Estimates that appeared in the media in the days that followed varied. One suggested four hundred, others fewer. There was no way of obtaining an exact count. The garden, though, was densely packed with people, and the excitement that they generated was intense.

The time to begin was approaching. Once the actors were in their costumes and the girls had finished putting on their makeup, Corinne joined everyone in the dressing room. She wore an ankle-length, dark blue Afghan dress covered in elaborate embroidery. With her dark hair and eyes, she could easily have been taken as an Afghan woman. She asked everyone to hold hands, close their eyes and take a deep breath.

"Open your eyes," she said after a moment. "Everyone say '*Merde!*' in one loud voice."

They did, even though they did not know what it meant.

"What is '*Merde?*'" Nabi asked.

She smiled. "It is French, it means 'shit.'"

"So we are now supposed to do a shitty performance?" Nabi asked incredulously.

"No, no, it is just a French tradition," Corinne reassured him. "We always say it before a performance."

"A weird tradition!" the actors exclaimed in a rare moment of total agreement.

The boys left to take their positions in a garden shed out of the sight of the audience. Everyone waited for the play to begin. Then it was 5:00 PM. Time to start.

:::::

The king and his nobles made their first appearance. As they entered, the audience immediately quieted. As they did, a donkey on the street outside the Foundation started braying loudly. Shah Mohammed had no choice but to say his opening lines. The audience broke out laughing as he tried to outshout the donkey. The other actors forced their jaws into a locked position to keep their composure. Finally, the donkey stopped, and Shah Mohammed looked triumphant, as if he had won a competition. Nabi, now as Sherzad, was the second actor to speak. A low rumble of approval rose from the Afghans as he took center stage. Here they were seeing Bulbul in real life.

The first joke came about two minutes into the script when Aref, now as Sohrab, suddenly realizes that the vow he has casually made to study for three years with the king also included a provision that he could not talk to women during that period. Somehow, he had missed that point. The look on Aref's face as he digested this unexpected news sent a wave of tentative laughter through the Afghans. They seemed undecided on whether they were meant to laugh out loud. But from that moment, they understood that the show was going to be funny. The foreigners, not understanding Dari, had no idea what Aref had said. However, they could tell from his face that it had been something humorous. They responded with the twitters of polite guests showing approval.

A few minutes later, the girls entered. A buzz went through the crowd. History was being made as women and men stood together on stage. For the Afghan men in the audience, especially the younger ones, seeing women like this was a rare experience, and something close to a thrill.

The audience, though, was also reacting to the girls' costumes, which looked rich and regal in the early evening light. The girls walked with dignity and grace as the swirls of fabric swept around them. Shahla Nawabi sat to one side scrutinizing the costumes, and nodding her approval.

Saba Sahar led the girls in at a stately pace, her artfully applied makeup completely intact, as she had always said it would be.

For those who had seen the production take shape, and been aware of the sometimes fractious rehearsals, nothing was more surprising than seeing Breshna moving with feminine airs and graces she had never before revealed. She was every inch a noble-woman, her tough policewoman's persona nowhere to be seen. The delicate way that she moved her hands, the shyness with which she smiled, the charm that she projected through her character were utterly unexpected. She had kept her mastery of the craft of acting as much a secret as her detective work.

No one in the cast was more transformed than Marina. Where was the giggling, frightened girl who had choked on her lines only a week before in rehearsal? Who was this elegant woman who moved with total assurance and spoke with the sophistication of someone ten years older? As the performance progressed, she seemed to grow into the role, exuding the self-confidence border-ing on hauteur that Shakespeare had intended.

The first moments the women were on stage were very formal, as the Princess of Herat explained her mission. She had come to settle an old financial dispute between her father in Herat and the King of Kabul. While that was going on, the boys tried hard not to reveal their immediate interest in the girls.

The verbal interplay between the king and the princess went smoothly, with more quiet ripples of Afghan laughter, especially as the women accompanying the princess confided their opinions of the men to one another. Then the banter between the men and women began with Aref, as Sohrab, addressing Marina, as Senober:

SOHRAB
Did not I see you dance in Kunduz once?

SENOBER
Did not I see you dance in Kunduz once?

SOHRAB
I know I did.

SENOBER
How needless was it then to ask the question!

The laughter from the Afghans in the audience was becoming more confident, more robust. Perhaps it was the inclusion of a reference to the northern Afghan city of Kunduz. Perhaps it was the unexpected snap-back from Marina to Aref's question. By the next scene, Aref's Sohrab was already trying to set up a secret rendezvous with Marina's Senober, with the help of Parwin's character, Fatima. The audience was eagerly waiting for their next funny line.

As the madcap efforts of the men to communicate with the women unobserved mounted, the shyness in the audience eased. At one point, Aref sought a hiding place by climbing a tree. Nabi then took refuge behind the same tree. Faisal ran around like a cat being chased by a dog, and ended up under the very same tree. Though he pulled a branch to cover his face, the rest of his body was plainly visible. And Shah Mohammed's serious-minded King of Kabul, when caught with amorous intentions of his own, first looked to his right and then to his left, then raced towards a flight of stairs.

Once the boys had discovered each other's schemes and decided to pursue the girls, the King of Kabul gave the battle cry: "Soldiers to the field!"

Big laugh.

While the laughs were one way to track the audience's interest, a look at their faces showed how intently they were engrossed in the story as it was unfolding. They all gave the appearance of being totally engaged, even the foreigners. They had been given a printed program that included a scene-by-scene synopsis in English. Many of them said later that while the synopsis was welcome, they had had no trouble following the story because of the clarity of the acting.

For one of the foreigners, though, one moment in the play brought a wrenching jolt. As the four noblewomen sat in front of their tent, their manservant, Kabir, served them tea in cups without handles. David instantly recognized the cups as his. He nearly jumped out of his seat and screamed, "Those are mine!" After the last performance, they were returned with thanks, and intact.

:·:·:·:

The show continued. Not one line was forgotten, which had been Corinne's biggest concern. Neither Kabir nor Parwin showed any hesitation or difficulty in remembering anything. Later, both said that running the entire show straight through had made things easier for them, instead of doing only a scene at a time, as in rehearsals.

The only distractions came from a few ringing mobile phones in the audience, the honking of the cars and buses from outside, the noise of military helicopters passing overhead and a child who wandered across the stage.

Midway through the performance, a nearby mosque called for evening prayers at sunset. A small number of men in the audience got up from where they were sitting. They went to the one end of the courtyard to an open area behind some tall rose bushes where there were no seats, as the roses blocked view. The men laid their head scarves out on the stone pavement, said their evening prayers, then headed back to their seats.

This created a problem as some of them came back through the playing area and climbed over the foreigners in the first row and the Afghans who had not prayed. When they got back to their chairs, a few found that their seats had been taken by others who had been standing at the back. The praying men whispered to the seat-grabbers in a threatening tone and demanded that the new arrivals get up.

In a country where some men stop to pray as soon as they hear the *azan* even if they are standing by the side of the road with traffic whizzing past them, it was not out of the ordinary for these men to break away from the performance for a few minutes to fulfill their religious obligations. Nor was it unusual that many other men chose not to pray at that time, but to wait until later, after the performance had ended.

::·:·:

As the early evening sunlight faded, a pair of floodlights that had been set up in the garden added a different quality to the light. It made the fabrics in the costumes, which had been eye-filling in the daylight, visually sumptuous.

Meanwhile, the kerosene lamps in the houses on the small mountain behind the Foundation were being lit. Their soft glow filled the windows of the countless mud-brick dwellings that perched in rows up the mountain. Youngsters were standing on their roofs, looking down into the Foundation's garden, trying to see what was going on. A couple of boys were flying kites over the audience's heads. The kids slowly disappeared as the darkness deepened. The lights in the houses twinkled like stars.

::·:·:

In due course it was time for the boys to appear as Indians, shirtless and wearing only *dhotis*, long panels of white cotton cloth wrapped around their waists then pulled through their legs. On their foreheads were red dots made with lipstick that they had rifled in a mad scramble through Breshna's handbag. No one had remembered to buy proper *bindi* powder from the Sikh shops that sold such things to Kabul's tiny Hindu community.

Nabi was the first to enter. The audience had not expected anything like this. Laughter erupted that only grew as Nabi started singing a well-known Bollywood song that everyone had heard for years, "Hey Ninee Gori, Hey Ninee Gori."

No sooner had he finished, than Faisal appeared, followed by Shah Mohammed and then Aref. Each one sang an equally well-known tune. All but Aref had good singing voices. The actors joked that Aref "does not have an ant's talent as a singer." That only made his song funnier. Everyone laughed at him more than the other boys because of how he tortured a song "that even babies can sing," as Afghans say.

The audience were out of their seats clapping, cheering, screaming. The sudden switch to Urdu had brought it all home. The Afghans no longer felt they had to be polite; they were having too much fun. The play was now about them. Not about Shakespeare. Not about kings. Not about princesses. Not about Taliban rules. This was the new Afghanistan, and it was happening right there in front of them, as comically-clad men sang outrageously funny songs to women seated with them on a stage, laughing themselves silly.

The foreigners, who probably did not know Urdu any more than they knew Dari, could not help but be caught up in the wildly joyous excitement all around them. They clapped and cheered with everyone else. The ten minutes or so that it took to play that scene was a living definition of euphoria.

For reasons only he knew, Faisal had come on in that the scene wearing a black T-shirt along with his *dhoti*. He wore the shirt inside out, but it was still possible to read the words "Pizza Hut" in reverse. It looked awful. Someone in the audience jokingly shouted in boisterous Afghan style, "Where is your tray of pizza?" It brought an extra guffaw, but not one the actors really wanted.

After the show, Faisal explained that he did not want the audience to see the large, ugly scars that he bore from the shrapnel wounds he had suffered on the night his five friends were killed. He wanted to be handsome. Understood. So, for the remaining performances, he found a way to tie his *dhoti* around his neck so that it not only covered the scars, but made his character look even funnier.

Now the actors could do no wrong. In the scene that followed, the boys one at a time chased the girls around the garden, and the audience went wild again, especially when Nabi chased Breshna. For many of the Afghans, it was Bulbul and Gul Chera as written by Shakespeare. Most of the Afghans who came to see the play thought their pairing had been deliberate.

Before the scene was over, four noble couples were poised to become four pairs of lovers. Actually, there were five couples.

Parwin's Fatima and Kabir's Sikander appeared to have developed an interest in each other as well. Though both were middle-aged, they had begun to act like teenagers, giving hints with their eyes of their growing interest in each other. That made everyone smile.

From the back of the audience, Corinne sat quietly watching the actors and feeling proud.

·:·:·:·

The same Mustafa Haidari who solved everyone's problems at the Foundation now entered the play briefly to resolve the issue of the vow taken by the four young nobles. Looking severe and handsome as a messenger from Herat, he arrived unexpectedly and ominously to announce that the father of the princess had died. The women must return home.

The sudden somber moment, so typical of Indian movies, provided a gentle transition out of the high jinks of the previous scenes and led to the parting of the couples as they agreed to meet again after one year. In the meantime, the women set tasks for the men. Marina, for instance, demanded that Aref take his wit to hospitals to cheer the sick, much to Aref's dismay.

·:·:·:·

Saba's Princess was never more riveting to watch than in her last scene as she dictates terms to the men. The smitten King of Kabul begs her to accept him.

HAROON, KING OF KABUL
Now, at the latest minute of the hour,
Grant us your loves.

PRINCESS OF HERAT
A time, methinks, too short
To make a world-without-end bargain in.

Her self-assured presence allowed no arguments. Several Afghan women in the audience could be seen to be nodding in approval. That is exactly what Corinne had wanted. That is every director's dream, to resonate with the audience. As Saba prepared to leave, the princess briefly takes the king's hand in hers. It was the first and only time that a man and a woman touched during the play. She initiated the action. It was unforced, and, in the end, unremarkable, because the actors had prepared the way for this moment so well. With that touch, one more small piece of Afghan history was made.

A moment later, the princess offered one of the best-known exit lines in all of Shakespeare.

PRINCESS OF HERAT
So now, you that way: we this way.

With wistful looks at the boys, the girls gathered up their skirts, and strolled out of the king's garden, leaving dented hearts full of promises and expectations. The audience did not wait for them to go. They jumped to their feet, clapping, cheering, shouting.

The boys tried to make their exit as directed from the side of the stage away from the girls, but the audience surrounded them. Both the boys and the girls returned to the stage. After bowing for several minutes, they sat down on the carpet-covered *takht* platform.

Nabi started playing the harmonium and singing a famous Afghan folk song. Everyone in the cast joined him, swaying from side to side. Many in the audience sang along. Corinne jumped to her feet and clapped along with everyone else. The moment had been unplanned, and was all the more powerful because of that.

:::::

More bows, more applause, and the actors ran off to their dressing room in the Foundation's old mansion. Before long, however, they were back in the garden greeting friends and relatives. The girls still wore their costumes, because everyone wanted to have their photos taken with them in their beautiful outfits.

Marina, who on so many days during rehearsals had never been far from a giggle, stood solemnly as several young men asked to be photographed with her. Their requests were formal; her response was pure *noblesse oblige* as she allowed them to stand next to her while someone focused the camera and snapped. All those appearances at film festivals had taught her how to maintain her composure while being admired and ogled.

As soon as the cameras had been put away, though, and the eager young men had left, she smiled again. It would not have looked decent for a young Afghan woman to be seen smiling in a photograph with men she did not know. Some boundaries had been crossed that night; others remained in place.

Parwin's husband, Tawab, was standing off to the side, basking in the glow of his wife's success. Dressed in a light-colored Western-style suit, he waited while Parwin and the other actors received the plaudits of the audience. Though few of the actors had met him, they immediately figured out who he was. His son and daughter, who stood next to him as enthralled as he was, had become the mascots of the production. The cast members introduced themselves, and congratulated him for Parwin's performance.

As the crowd thinned, the cast and their relatives moved into one of the Foundation's large rooms, where food had been set out on a long cloth laid on the floor, and Afghan *rabab* music was spreading its twangy joy from a CD player. Everyone settled themselves on *toshaks* as they ate and talked about the evening. Corinne was exuberant. Nabi had a look of contentment that had not often been seen from him. And the interpreter was happy that his job was nearly over.

:::::

That night, Afghan television networks such as TOLO TV and Afghan National Television talked about the play during and after the evening news, which made many people curious about what was happening at the Foundation. The next evening, nearly a thousand people stood in the street wanting to be in the audience. Though the Foundation had greatly increased the number of seats from the night before, there were still not nearly enough.

Corinne was concerned that a riot outside the gate could cause problems for the actors. She went to the entrance, and tried to stop the incoming flow. "Tell them they cannot come in," she told the doorkeeper in her most commanding voice. "We have no seats left. We are full. Tell them to please come back tomorrow night," she implored.

The doorkeeper, a pleasant middle-aged man, smiled, but people kept pushing past him, with a couple of hundred more well-dressed Afghans, both men and women, still in the street trying to get in. Finally, the thick wooden door to the Foundation was eased shut, to shouts of disapproval from those outside. They continued to mill around for some time, though, expecting that the doors would open after a while and let more in. To the regret of all, they did not.

:::::

At the first performance, most of the Afghans in the audience were men. When they saw that there was nothing anti-Islamic or un-Islamic in the play, they came back on subsequent evenings and brought their wives and daughters to see it.

Just before the third performance was to begin, several women in burqas led by a young man entered the garden. They made their way down the stairway that led from the entrance to the grass, then found a place to sit in a far corner. They sat there quietly, pulling the burqas away from their faces whenever Marina came on stage. They hung on her every word. Their eyes filled with laughter at her many jokes, but they never made a sound. They looked at each other and shared their joy, but only among themselves. They were Marina's mother and sisters, led by one of her brothers. Their pride in Marina was plainly evident. As soon as the performance ended, they glided back up the staircase, and out the door.

From one performance to the next, Marina had been finding new depth in her role as Senober. She finally understood what it meant to do theater. The lines that had once so terrified her now propelled her into an immediate rapport with her audience.

"I love theater," she said to the interpreter after the fourth performance. "As much as I enjoy the poetry of Shakespeare, I enjoy the reactions of the audience more. Shakespeare's lines and the audience are interlinked. The more I say my lines with confidence, the more the audience applaud me. They probably think I put those words together. Poor Shakespeare! He wrote this beautiful play and people like me get credit for it. He should be known worldwide. Do people know who he is?"

"Maybe some do," the interpreter said with a hint of a smile.

The Queen's Palace

Kabul. 4 September 2005.

For four nights as they performed at the Foundation, the excitement grew among the actors. The unrestrained enthusiasm for their production in the Afghan media along with their audiences' vociferous response after every performance was overwhelming. None of them had expected it.

"This is what doing theater is about," Corinne told any of them who would listen. "You have the opportunity to connect directly with your audience. You can't do that in film."

Always in the backs of their minds hung the knowledge that before their production was finished, they would be taking the excitement they were creating to the garden of the emperor.

∷∷∷

After the last performance at the Foundation, the job of moving *Love's Labour's Lost* to the Bagh-e Babur started immediately. The costumes were packed, the props were gathered and put in boxes, and the carpets that had covered the *takht* of the king were rolled and stacked.

Early the next morning, the interpreter along with Mustafa Haidari, the smiling solver of all problems, organized a team of workers from the Foundation to move everything, including the chairs. Mustafa "gave orders with sweet words," as Afghans say, and made his crew happy to be working with him.

The interpreter had not been back to the Bagh-e Babur since the evening when he had gone there with Corinne and the others. As he walked with Mustafa through the covered arcade and onto the terrace of the Queen's Palace, he was amazed to see that the garden and the buildings around it had been utterly transformed by Jolyon Leslie's workers. Gone were the piles of rubble, the ladders and the buckets of mud. Instead, long sheets of burlap had been spread over the wet stucco on the walls so that it would dry evenly. More burlap hung between the arches, giving a tattered grandeur to the ruins.

The remains of the old fountain, which had appeared so ugly only a few weeks ago, had entirely vanished, as Jolyon had said they would. Mustafa's crew started setting out row after row of white chairs where the fountain had been, forming wide arcs. The Queen's Palace lacked the well-tended grass of the Foundation's lawn, so four large Hazaragi *kilims* were laid on the hard earth to create a performance area in front of the terrace's battlements. One of them was the same *kilim* on which everyone had sat during the first workshop. It had become a kind of totem for the actors, accompanying them through their journey with Corinne.

To one side, Hashmat Ghani's six-sided tent was raised. Its fanciful presence stood as a hint that something wonderful was going to happen there.

"We have at least twice as many chairs as at the Foundation," Mustafa stated proudly. "And there are more coming from some chair rental companies which do weddings. Nobody is going to be left outside tonight." He asked the workers to lay out a line of *toshaks* in front of the first row of chairs. He wanted anyone sitting on the ground with their legs crossed to be comfortable.

No tickets had been distributed, so no one had any idea who might show up, or how many. Several diplomats and other notables had accepted an invitation to attend a reception hosted by the British Council following the performance. The rest were a complete unknown.

∷∷∷

The actors arrived by midday. They worked with Corinne to adapt their blocking to this entirely new setting. The garden at the Foundation was small, offering many places for the actors to hide behind bushes or in small rooms when they were not on stage. At the Queen's Palace, everything was exposed. There was no tree for Aref to climb.

Despite the heat, the actors worked without the usual complaints to solve the problems the new space presented. The boys would enter down the grand staircase stage right of the battlements. They would wait for their cue out of sight in one of the rooms still under construction. That meant that they had to be in position before the audience was let in. The girls would await their entrance at the far side of the terrace and descend the other stairs stage left.

There were no clearly marked walkways in the garden as there had been at the Foundation. They were important for the scene late in the play during which each of the boys one by one chases the girl of his dreams through the audience. Getting the scene right required a delicate balance. The boys' feelings had to be playful, with no hint of force. The girls had to make it clear that they welcomed the boys' pursuit, while still observing Afghan norms for female decorum.

The scene had worked well in the previous performances, coming as it did after the whirlwind of good humor that had blown in with the Indians. At the Bagh-e Babur, the interpreter had to work out the chase routes with the actors so they could run around the white chairs and get back to the performance area when they should.

The decisions being made might have brought fevered arguments a week earlier. The success of the four performances at the Foundation, however, had melded the actors into a company. They were living up to Nabi's boast back in April, "We could challenge the whole country."

:::::

After a walk-through of the whole show to make sure everyone knew where they were meant to be, the actors broke for lunch. Large trays of rice cooked with lamb, raisins and shredded carrots arrived, and were carried to the rooms surrounding the ornate marble *hamam*. The actors were using the small chambers connected to it as dressing rooms and a place to hang out until the performance began. They gathered around the trays of food.

Some of the girls were seated in a circle on the floor of the *hamam* itself, dishing out *pelau* and *kebab*, the mainstays of every Afghan picnic. When an American visitor arrived, Faisal exploded with "My best friend!" thereby exhausting his English vocabulary while dispensing a bear hug.

"I have lived all my life in Kabul," Parwin enthused, "yet I have never been to the Queen's Palace before today. It was always closed to the public. I am so proud that despite the war and chaos over the past three decades, all these things survived, this marble *hamam* and those stones engraved with poems."

:::::

The atmosphere was electric. The actors were ready. It would be three hours before they finally marched out onto the stage, but the anticipation that they were generating was palpable. All the costumes were hanging neatly on a rack.

When everyone had had enough to eat, the singing started, led by Daoud. Though Daoud had the good looks of a Bollywood movie star, he could never pass a screen test. He froze when a camera was pointed at him. He was by nature an entertainer, though not one who would put himself in front of others to seek their applause. Rather, he unobtrusively positioned himself amid his audience, and got them to be part of whatever song he was singing. As the dishes were being picked up, Daoud started a song, and within seconds had the rest of them singing along with him.

Then came the dancing. The girls went to an adjacent room, out of sight of the men, and whooped and laughed as they stretched out their arms in the sinuous moves and tiny steps that the women in their families had been doing for centuries. And if some of the men happened to catch sight through the open door, well, they were all a kind of family now. No one would have defended the honor of those actresses more vigorously than the actors.

:.:.:.

It was still too early for the actors to put on their costumes, and too late to go anywhere. So they settled for a walk around the trees and grass in Babur's magnificent garden outside the Queen's Palace. Daoud went with them. Then in his early thirties, he was nonetheless filled with a young man's enthusiasm for anything new he encountered. That day, he saw Babur's pool for the first time.

Maybe it was actually Abdur Rahman's pool. Some king had built it. Daoud was determined to be in it. It was twice the size of an Olympic pool, with steps leading down the slope of the hill into its dark water. Daoud had no interest in the steps. Though modesty is deeply ingrained in Afghans, the sight of the water freed Daoud from all inhibitions. He rapidly pulled off his knee-length *kameez* shirt and undid the knotted belt that held up his *shalwar* trousers. He stepped out of his sandals as the *shalwar* fell down around his ankles in a pair of crumpled cotton rings. Wearing only his blue boxer shorts, he spread his arms towards the water, as if offering it a hug, laughed and then made a perfect dive into its dust-clouded depths.

Few Afghans have a chance to learn to swim in their arid country. Some might have gone to the man-made Qargha Lake just outside Kabul, or taken a dip in the stunningly azure lakes of Band-e-Amir in central Afghanistan, but most had not. The large municipal swimming pools built by the Communists had not held water for nearly a generation. Yet there was Daoud, when he finally resurfaced, executing all kinds of strokes, with his ever-luminescent smile.

"Take a picture," shouted this most camera-shy of Afghans. As the interpreter did so, he guessed that this was going to be a moment Daoud would remember long after everything else that had happened during his brush with Shakespeare had begun to fade.

:::::

The interpreter made his way back to the *hamam* complex and stretched out on the cool marble floor in its innermost room. It was quiet and far from the actors. He had been up early to work with Mustafa on the chairs and the tent, and had been kept busy by Corinne and the actors out in the heat. He needed a rest before the show started in an hour. As he drifted off into a nap, he could hear the actors in the other rooms, singing, joking and drinking tea.

From time to time, Faisal's voice joined with the rest of the boys. Daoud, now back in the *hamam*, cheered him on. Faisal was always the first to put on his costume. Then he picked up his script and held it in his hand as if it were part of his outfit. He read his lines over and over, along with everyone else's, as he walked around and checked on everyone.

He teased the girls for a few minutes, then walked into the room where the interpreter was nearly asleep. "Are you awake?" he asked in a whispery voice.

The interpreter opened his eyes a little, and looked up. "What is it, Faisal jan?" he asked in a tired voice.

Faisal came and stood over him. "I've been reading the whole script in the past few days, many times," he said.

"That's good. Perhaps you can tell me more about it later," the interpreter said.

"I will, because the more I read it, the more it charms me." Faisal sat down next to the interpreter. "I had no idea how deep this play is when I first read the script. It is like Rumi and Hafez; it works on you after you digest it." He was talking softly, as if he were worried he would disturb someone.

"Did it take you so long to digest it?" the interpreter asked. "What would you do if you had eaten old camel meat?" He was hoping a joke would send him away.

"No, no, I'm serious!" Faisal's whispery voice was making hoarse echoes in the domed white room. He leaned closer. "I really feel these words now as I say them. I really feel them. I've never read such a powerful script before. I don't think everybody in the group really understands the deepest meanings of these lines. I think they just say the words, because we're actors, and this is what we do. But now I really know what they mean."

"This is good to hear," the interpreter said to him as he yawned. "Now, please let me rest for a while. I'm exhausted. I'll have a lot to do in half an hour. We will talk about all this another time."

"All right, all right. Have your rest," Faisal whispered, and got up to leave. Then, just as he was going through the arched door, Faisal turned and said quietly, "I've heard that many Afghans have gone to live in England. I think Shakespeare was one of them."

⁙⁙⁙

It was nearly time to start. The boys were adjusting their costumes. The girls were taking last looks in the mirror to check their makeup. Breshna handed her lipstick to Nabi so no one would have to go plundering her handbag for it when they came to the Indian scene.

Nabi said, "Thank you, Breshna jan," and pretended for a second to use it on his lips.

Breshna made a rancid smile at him. "You idiot," she said.

Her back was turned to a window that looked onto the terrace. As she turned, she caught sight of a man with a long bushy beard peering in at her. Breshna screamed, "There's a Talib!" The women panicked and ran out of the room into the hallway, which had no windows, shouting, "Taliban! Taliban!"

The men ran to the door where the found the bearded man standing apologetically. He said he was not a Talib, but a construction worker. He was just curious to know what was happening inside the rooms where he had been working all week. The man left. Everyone calmed down. Breshna, though, was shaken, and until the performance started, she kept repeating, "What if the Taliban attack us?"

Parwin told her to stop being silly. Always in the back of all the actors' minds, however, was the sad truth that they were easy targets.

::::::

Just before the doors to the Queen's Palace were opened for the audience, Corinne gathered the company together for what had become a nightly pre-performance ritual. They closed their eyes, took a deep breath, opened their eyes and shouted, "*Merde!*" For most, this was the only French word they knew. It echoed through the domed chambers of the *hamam*.

The boys excitedly scampered across the terrace. A holding room had been created for them in the other wing by draping large sheets of burlap in a few key places. The doors to the Queen's Palace swung open, and the great and the good of Kabul began to enter.

A Night in the Emperor's Garden

Kabul. 5 September 2005.

As the incoming theater-goers emerged from the covered passage and stepped into the Queen's Palace courtyard, many paused in astonishment at what they saw. It was unlike any other public space in Kabul.

Several members of the family of Afghanistan's last king, Zahir Shah, were among them. Though the Queen's Palace had once been owned by their family, few of them had ever been there. They walked around the terrace and the courtyard, taking in all the details and enjoying the view of the mountains through the arched openings in the western wall.

The ambassadors of France and Canada arrived, as did a number of Cabinet ministers and other government officials, some with their families. Businessmen from Kabul and staff from international aid projects came as well. One of them brought a group of Afghan teachers from Kandahar, Farah, Laghman and Kunduz provinces – all very conservative areas. None had ever attended a play before.

As the time for the performance neared, a wave of Afghan workmen from the Bagh-e Babur came in and took seats along the edge of the side terrace from where they could watch the audience as clearly as the actors. Others sat on the steps of the grand staircases. Some had brought their children.

More came. They filled the side terraces. Some came down and sat in the chairs. The performance's starting time came and went. It had to be delayed as the flood of people kept rolling in through the arcade, some from the houses built by squatters on the mountain behind the Queen's Palace. Mustafa and his crew located additional chairs and arranged them behind the others. Some in the audience chose to stand, and in some places they were three-deep behind the rows of chairs. As Mustafa had promised, there was room for everyone.

Finally, with the stucco of the palace reflecting a golden red from the setting sun, the play began. As the actors emerged into the garden of the emperor, they instinctively understood that they were making history in a place where so much earlier Afghan history had also been made.

:::::

With a great sense of authority, the King of Kabul came forth from the boys' holding room, strode across the terrace and made his way down the wide stone stairs. He mounted his carpet-covered *takht* and slowly surveyed the crowd, just as a real king might. The audience responded with utter silence, as if they were truly in a royal presence.

Shah Mohammed had been a king for four nights now. He had begun to enjoy being the most important man in the story, even more important than his teacher and friend Nabi, at least for these few hours during the play. He drew himself up and spoke the first line announcing the vow that he and his friends had made.

Corinne had worked with the actors that afternoon on projecting their voices. Earlier she had expressed her concern to the interpreter that coming from the relatively compact quarters of the Foundation's garden, they would have trouble being heard across the wide expanses of the palace courtyard. As the performance started, the interpreter positioned himself at the back of those standing. Every word Shah Mohammed said could be heard crisply and clearly. The interpreter gave a thumbs-up to Corinne, who was seated in the first row of chairs. She smiled back, looking happy.

As Shah Mohammed finished his speech, the boys ceremoniously made their way down the stairs in single file to join him. Their formal entrance entranced the audience. Stylized processions, even a small one like this one, are uncommon in Afghan culture.

The first joke was coming soon. Over the course of the previous performances, the actors had learned that the response to that first joke closely predicted the reaction of the audience for the rest of the play. If the audience laughed shyly, they would grin at the other jokes but repress any real laughter. If they chuckled audibly, then they would probably laugh a little louder every time until fully unleashing their laughter during the scene with the Indians.

The joke came. Aref said his line, and gave his look of astonishment. All the workmen up on the terraces, on the steps and standing around the perimeter exploded in laughter. That ignited the Afghans in the seats who might have felt more restrained, but now clapped, laughed and looked at each other in delight, and laughed some more. The eyes of the actors sparkled. They had never had an echoing response like this. Then the audience instantly grew quiet, as they hung on every word, until they erupted even more loudly with the next joke, even though it was not as funny as the first one.

:::::

The girls entered. No one, however, could really call them girls anymore, not with the profound dignity with which they were all carrying themselves. As they descended the other flight of stairs with exceptional poise, they and their costumes had never looked more exquisite. Perhaps a grand arrival by the ladies on camels would have been more theatrical, but it could not have been more spectacular. As always, a sense that something remarkable was happening fell over the crowd as the women joined the men on stage.

Parwin was astonished as she came down the grand staircase behind the ladies. "I was not expecting to see so many women in the audience, especially foreigners," she said later. "There were three times as many people as at the previous performances at the Foundation. Actors perform better when they have a large audience."

:::::

Perhaps it came from being in the emperor's garden, or maybe because they had a larger crowd, but all the actors were in top form that night. None had so completely inhabited their roles before as they did in this performance. Parwin and Kabir, as the hapless go-betweens for the noblemen and noblewomen, were flawless. They drew big laughs for their comic business, which had never worked so well before.

Saba and Breshna, who by day were enforcers of the law in an often lawless land, exuded a presence that resonated with the protocols of the ancient court of Herat, long the seat of learning and the arts in Afghanistan.

Marina giggled only on cue, and was deeply moving when she meant to be. Her work in films had taught her how to draw focus by being still. Leila's mock swooning over Faisal's Mansour adroitly pushed the comedy to the edge of the absurd. She towered over him, and that made it all funnier.

Faisal's gift for guileless hamming was her perfect foil. He made his character self-important without ever becoming that way himself. Perhaps because he had so many self-doubts.

Aref was especially electrifying. Instead of hiding in a tree, as he had at the Foundation, he somehow managed to climb inside one of the towering arches. He loomed above the other actors in the garden far below, reacting with amazement at their clumsy efforts to hide. It was hard for the audience to take their eyes off him. Throughout the rest of the evening, he glowed with an energy that made him more spellbinding than he had ever been before.

As the actors performed, first one, then another, and another youngster began to appear on the perimeter wall behind the terrace and its arches. How had they gotten up there? The wall was easily twenty feet above the street. Had someone brought a ladder? That wall had been built by kings to keep armies out, yet these kids, like human kites, had managed to fly themselves to the top of it. They were probably too far away to hear the actors, but the roar of the crowd kept them transfixed. Behind them, as had happened at the Foundation, the mud houses on the hills began to turn on their lights. This neighborhood had electricity, though at a low voltage. The soft light of underpowered, unshaded bulbs glowed through a thousand windows.

Meanwhile, the floodlights that had been placed around the courtyard were beginning to isolate the playing area from its surroundings as it replaced the fading daylight. This had the effect of drawing the audience ever more deeply into the story. The colors in the four *kilims* and the carpets on the *takht* took on an extra richness against the dust and the stone battlements. With the deepening darkness, an ever-growing number of workmen came and sat on the grand staircases. Before long, the steps were filled as if they had been designed as a grandstand.

By the time the Indian scene started, it was fully dark and the actors looked like rock stars in megawatt stage lighting. The audience went wild the moment Nabi appeared. That night he had fastened his *dhoti* with a safety pin to keep it from slipping off, as it nearly had two nights before, leaving him grabbing its cotton lengths to cover his plaid boxer shorts.

Nabi began to sing, and the audience made so much noise that few could really hear him at all. Applause for Nabi was like a drug. The more he heard, the more exuberant his performance became. The song went on for several extra verses. When Faisal followed him, they cheered even more. And so it went. No one could hear how bad a singer Aref was that night. As soon as he started his song, the audience started singing with him. In the impromptu gallery along the side terraces, workmen in the audience were dancing with their arms flung out and their hands in the air.

By now all those standing were pushing forward. They wanted to hear and see everything better, to be part of things. The neat aisles that had been laid out where the men could chase the women were completely clogged. With the chase scene coming, an effort was made to move enough people out of the way so that the performers could run through the crowd and get back to the playing area. No one wanted to move.

Nabi and Breshna were the first to run. Perhaps because they were so well known to so many in the audience, the standees instinctively opened a path for them. As they raced towards the back of the audience, Daoud waited for them, making big gestures pointing to their left so they would know where to go. They were moving too fast to stop and ask directions. For a short distance, he ran alongside them, guiding them through the crowd and back towards the stage.

The audience was as energized by the chases as they had been by the Indian scene. The workmen up on the terraces were shouting at the running couples as if they were placing bets on some kind of race or dog fight.

While all this was going on, Parwin stood on stage concerned about her daughter, who was wandering among the audience. "I was looking for her from the corners of my eyes. I noticed a foreigner woman kissing her on the check. Then my daughter pointed at me on the stage and told them that I was her mother. The blonde lady smiled at me. I smiled back at her, but it happened at a time when I was supposed to look sad. Quickly I tried to frown. It was when the princess received the message about her father's death. A few people in the audience may have noticed me smiling, but I think the rest were all focused on Saba Sahar."

With the dramatic arrival of Mustafa Haidari as the messenger from Herat, the mood changed, and the play entered its quieter final minutes. The audience seemed to be relieved to have a rest from the exuberant laughter. They listened carefully as the men expressed their affection and intentions for the women, and as the women gently deflected them, at least for one year. And then the final line: "So now, you that way: we this way."

The girls walked from the playing area and up the grand stairs to an ear-shattering roar of approval from the crowd of a kind that they may never hear again. Hundreds and hundreds of clapping hands and cheering voices. The boys were blocked from leaving, as the stairs down which they had first entered was now entirely filled by spectators. So they stood there smiling until the women returned to take a bow. And another bow. And another bow. And another. The audience did not want to let them go.

As they had done at the Foundation, the actors then sat on the *takht* platform and sang a few Afghan songs. More clapping. More cheering. More singing, until finally they were able to make their way back up to the *hamam* and their dressing room. Under those elaborately plastered domes, they shrieked their delight and hugged one another. None of them had ever experienced anything like this before.

They started singing. Indian songs. Afghan songs. Beatles songs. Any kind of song they knew, as they hung their costumes back on the racks.

Aref was aglow. "Shakespeare is an amazing writer. He wrote as if he were aware of humanity's pain, and always had a simple answer to man's problems. When I said my lines, I felt as if they were mine. Sometimes they were bitter and sharp, sometimes they were sweet, smooth and soothing. It was my first time to be in a play and do Shakespeare. What an honor!"

∷∵∷

At the lower end of the garden, the tall doors in the Queen's Palace gatehouse swung open to save the audience from having to climb the grand stairs to the terrace to exit through the covered passage. Many seemed to want to do that anyway, to extend for a few more minutes the sense of enchantment that had been created there that night.

Slowly the audience filed out into the magnificent gardens that Babur had laid out so carefully only a few decades before Shakespeare had written *Love's Labour's Lost*.

:::::

Corinne was happier than anyone in Kabul had ever seen her. She was receiving congratulations from all sides. Despite all the obstacles, she had somehow managed to will this unlikely creature called *Love's Labour's Lost* into existence, and then drive it to success.

:::::

A week before the first performance, Andrew North of the BBC had interviewed members of the cast. His report aired on BBC Worldwide television on the morning of the performance at the Bagh-e Babur. It was widely seen by the international community in Kabul and probably motivated many of them to come, including many journalists.

One of them, from London's *Daily Telegraph*, quoted Faisal saying the Taliban would "never allow us to put on a play, to tell a story about love. Now we have a democracy, and we can show these things to our people. I am so proud." That was a message that resonated. Shakespeare in Kabul was suddenly political and a hot news story.

The Associated Press published a story that was republished on September 8th by newspapers on every continent except Antarctica. That same day, BBC World Service radio aired a story about the production which was heard even in Antarctica. Seven continents in one day. Not bad.

The Associated Press story captured the visceral excitement felt by Afghans, who saw the production as a celebration of the end of the Taliban era: "It's hardly a tale the Taliban would have approved, but judging by the cheers and whoops, many in the audience did."

A few days later, the serious British weekly magazine *The Economist* waxed poetic about the production, headlining it, "a magic performance in a dusty Afghan garden," and describing it as a "wonderful production." Reporter James Astill concluded his unexpected turn as a drama critic with a prescience born of his

regular assignment as *The Economist's* defence and security corre-
spondent: "In Afghanistan as in Shakespeare's comedies, the future
is less rosily settled than it may seem. As it is said in *Love's Labour's
Lost*: 'Worthies, away! The scene begins to cloud.'"

"The Scene Begins to Cloud"

Encores

Kabul, September 2005–April 2006.

Even before that final glorious evening at the Bagh-e Babur, there was already talk about additional performances. Several government ministers had seen the production. Some had come back for a second look with their families. A few of them said that they wanted to bring *Love's Labour's Lost* to their ministries so their workers could enjoy it, especially the women who were not as free to attend a public event. The Minister of Women's Affairs was especially eager, saying, "I want my people to see what Afghans can do."

In the end, however, no additional performances took place that year. Afghanistan's first parliamentary elections were about to be held. There were widespread concerns of violence in the run-up to the voting. Public performances, especially of a show funded by foreigners, were seen as possible targets. Also, the holy month of Ramazan would start soon after the elections. No performances could be given until it had ended. By then, cool weather and shorter days would make outdoor shows problematic.

Planning turned quickly to doing something the following year.

:::::

Corinne prepared to leave for Paris amid hugs and tears from her cast. Marina was inconsolable. She sobbed, saying over and over, "You are my director," while hanging on to her, as if trying to keep her from going to the airport. Even Nabi, who had never hesitated to challenge Corinne on just about anything, was now describing her as a "great director, a wonderful woman. She is my good friend."

:::::

The interpreter relished his release from the pressures of getting all the actors together every day, listening to everyone's complaints and seeing that Corinne had everything she needed. Then he found he had one last unexpected chore.

For the next several weeks, a steady stream of university students who had seen the play wanted to know everything they could about *Love's Labour's Lost*. They had little or no idea who Shakespeare was. Like all Afghans, they were hungry for knowledge. They came to the Foundation looking for copies of the play. The Foundation referred them to the interpreter.

They asked to read the Dari script for *Love's Labour's Lost*. A copy was given to one young man, who photocopied it. Then he photocopied his photocopy to give to a friend, who photocopied that one. Another guy photocopied that one, and gave it to someone else. Over the next few weeks, so many copies of copies had been made that it had become almost impossible to decipher the words.

When asked why he liked Shakespeare so much, one of the young men said, "Shakespeare makes you laugh in one eye, and cry in the other."

:::::

The British Council was pleased with the production and agreed to underwrite additional performances the next year in Kabul, as well as a tour to Herat and Mazar-e-Sharif. Other donors were approached. The Canadian embassy offered to contribute $500, but never actually did. The American embassy declined since Shakespeare was not an American writer.

Corinne returned to Kabul in early May 2006. She reunited the cast for a picnic in the garden at the old fort, where she was again staying. Several carpets had been laid in the grass in the shade of a large tree. Platters of food were brought out. Nabi played the harmonium and declaimed *ghazals*, the great lyric poems of the Indo-Persian world. Shah Mohammed accompanied him on a *tabla*. Everyone sang. It was a good beginning.

Over the next few days, however, Corinne learned that Marina was committed to making a film near Bamyan that summer, and Saba Sahar had to go to Germany to raise funds for her film company. Corinne had to find two new actresses.

Breshna's teenage daughter, Wajma, had seen every performance and many rehearsals the year before. She knew nearly everyone's lines. Though she was a little shy, in the way all Afghan girls are taught to be, Corinne sensed that Wajma's years of exposure to her mother's performing career had given her skills that were not immediately apparent.

"Would you be interested in taking over the role that was played by Marina?" Corinne asked her one day.

Wajma was stunned and could barely say anything. "My mother is the actress in my family, not me," she replied. "I'll have to think about it."

While she did, Corinne asked her to read Marina's lines during rehearsals. It was a subtle ploy, and it worked.

"That night, I took my mother's script and read the whole play in my room," Wajma said. "After the first line, I could not stop. Of course, I did not understand everything, yet the poetry was so rich, so enchanting and beautiful. I could not resist, as the words made me stand up, and I said them out loud to the walls in my room as if they were the other characters and would respond back to me. The next day when I woke up, I asked myself, 'Why not?'"

Within a few days, Wajma was a full member of the cast.

The search for an actress to assume Saba's role as the Princess of Herat was more complicated. Corinne met with several. None seemed to be right. Briefly she considered performing the part herself, if no one else could be found. Finally, she encountered Amina Jaffari, who had appeared in many Afghan television programs and films, and looked the part of a noblewoman. She proved to be a quick study, even of Shakespeare's poetry.

Nabi did another walkout, as he had the year before. Corinne shrugged off his departure and said he would come back. She went on rehearsing without him. Two days later, he returned. There was no time to waste talking about whatever had annoyed him. He rejoined the rehearsals as if he had been there all along.

Then a day of rehearsals was lost quite unexpectedly owing to a tragic incident that led to anti-foreigner riots on May 28. The brakes on an American military vehicle failed while it was coming down a steep hill on the outskirts of Kabul, and it had ploughed into a crowd of shoppers near a large open-air bazaar at Khair Khana, killing several Afghans. When an angry crowd surrounded the truck, some of the soldiers inside panicked and opened fire. As word spread across the city, mobs materialized and randomly attacked buildings that evoked the presence of foreigners, from Chinese brothels and CARE International's compound to a pizza shop, though it was owned by Afghans.

The riots created a tense atmosphere in Kabul for several days afterwards. To many people, they were the first tangible indication that things in Afghanistan were deteriorating. The glow of that special evening in the garden of the emperor still hung in the air for those who had been there. With the riots, though, no one could pretend that the reality on the ground was not changing.

Afghans felt deep dismay as they watched the government of President Hamid Karzai become increasingly corrupt, and the American development and military effort prove astonishingly inept. Some of the men who had been drawn to join the Taliban a decade earlier decided to regroup. Encouraged by backers in Pakistan, they started using suicide bombings and other terror tactics that previously had been unknown in Afghanistan.

The first performance, held once again in the garden of the Foundation, was a bit shaky, as Amina and Wajma felt their way through their roles. Though Wajma was very good, she had never performed publicly before. She spoke softly, timidly, and froze for a moment when the girls exchanged their headscarves with one another to mislead the boys.

"I was standing there in front of the men in the audience without my headscarf," she said later. "It was only for a few seconds, but I was very self-conscious and uncomfortable. I had never done that before."

Some of the other actors stumbled once or twice as well. Probably no one in the audience was aware of any problem, but the missed cues and fluffed lines put the actors on alert. They knew that they had a huge reputation to live up to.

At a performance in the courtyard of the old fort where Corinne was staying, the actors performed around a large fountain David had built. The interpreter devised a comic moment in which Shah Mohammed as the King of Kabul showed his displeasure with Nabi and Faisal by dunking their heads into the fountain. Corinne had said it was "vulgar," and was opposed to it. Maybe it was vulgar, but the actors did it anyway, and the audience roared, among them Prince Mirwais, the youngest son of the former king, Zahir Shah.

That was the second time the prince had attended the play. He had seen it a few nights earlier at the Foundation, but had to leave immediately afterwards to have dinner with his father at the Arg, as the king's palace is called. He had called his driver more than an hour before to arrange a pick-up. It was still rush hour, and the traffic was in total gridlock. Many streets had recently been narrowed, as one embassy and international organization after another erected huge cement bollards in front of their properties to deflect the impact of car bombs. His driver was stuck somewhere.

Prince Mirwais pleaded for someone to find him a car that would get him to the Arg quickly. The interpreter beckoned to Daoud and introduced him to the prince, explained the situation to him, and instructed him, "Daoud, be Daoud."

Prince Mirwais asked what that meant, and was told, "As you will soon see, sir. Daoud is the fastest driver in Kabul, and he is at his very best in rush hour."

The Prince looked hopeful, but unconvinced. He asked Daoud, "Can we get to the Arg in ten minutes?" It was no great distance.

Daoud looked at Prince Mirwais, and said with his ever-luminous smile, "Of course. Let's go, and not waste time." Prince Mirwais smiled too, and appeared to relax a bit. Daoud had that effect, even on princes.

They left. Seven minutes later, Prince Mirwais called the interpreter, "You really do have the fastest driver in Kabul. I'm home already. Can Daoud be my driver when you no longer need him?"

Prince Mirwais suggested to his father that the actors be invited to perform in the garden of the Arg so the king could see the play. Zahir Shah, then ninety-three years old, was no longer officially the King of Afghanistan, as the monarchy had been abolished. He had been given the title "Father of the Nation," but was generally called "the king" by most Afghans.

Zahir Shah said he would be happy to welcome the actors to the Arg. Unfortunately, his health declined soon after, and it became impossible. The royal endorsement of the production, however, added an element of glamour.

:::::

In all, there were five performances in Kabul that second year, with three at the Foundation, one at the old fort and one in the emperor's garden, although not in the Queen's Palace. Instead, it was staged in the caravanserai that had been under construction the year before. The caravanserai's courtyard was ideal for the play, being both grand and intimate. More importantly, it could provide a higher level of security than the Queen's Palace. Things that had not been an issue the year before suddenly were.

A few days later, the actors were all set to fly to Herat to start their tour. Several performances had been scheduled, with one in the ancient Citadel that once had been sacked by Tamburlaine, the same tyrant depicted by Shakespeare's contemporary, Christopher Marlowe. With an ironic echo of present-day Afghanistan, Marlowe was later charged with blasphemy, and then mysteriously murdered.

Aref noted philosophically, "Last year we performed in the garden of Babur, who built many things. This year we are doing the play in the place where Tamburlaine destroyed many things. Is this some of kind of a sign for something bad that might happen to us?"

No one answered. Their optimism of the year before was fading. The riot, the suicide bombers, the barbed wire and high cement bollards guarding foreign and governmental organizations were making Kabul feel like a war zone again.

∷∷

Herat is a remarkable city that is unlike any other in Afghanistan. At many times in its history it has been part of various Persian empires. Its gardens, its covered bazaars, its silk industry, its food and its accent all retain a distinctly Persian quality. Herat province borders Iran. That simple geopolitical fact causes its leaders to be careful.

Indeed, the day before the actors were set to depart from Kabul, the Governor of Herat, Sayed Hossein Anwari, unexpectedly raised objections and forbade the performances. He had never heard of Shakespeare. What he knew was that the actors were proposing to have women appear on stage in front of an audience that included men.

Phone calls were made to the Governor's office to plead the actors' case. By chance it was learned that he had come to Kabul for the weekend. Leila mentioned that her father was a good friend of the Governor and offered to arrange a meeting with him, as a result of which the Governor welcomed a *Love's Labour's Lost* delegation into his home. Many cups of green tea were drunk as the play was described. The Governor said he would decide whether to grant permission in a few days.

∷∷∷

With the actors all packed and ready to travel, the itinerary was changed and they headed for Mazar-e-Sharif first instead. They would go to Herat later, if the Governor allowed.

The actors were pumped up as they piled into a pair of Kabul–Mazar highway taxi vans that the Foundation had hired for them. Leila's brother, Nazeef, joined them. She was unmarried; it would have been improper for her to travel without a male relative.

The company of *Love's Labour's Lost* was at last going to "challenge the whole country" – and on their own. With the security situation deteriorating, Corinne was staying in Kabul. She was concerned for her safety. The interpreter took over as their director and tour manager. "Let's go," he told the drivers, and they headed north.

Mazar-e-Sharif

Mazar-e-Sharif. May 2006.

The eight-hour drive to Mazar crosses the Hindu Kush mountains through the Salang Tunnel, then winds across the broad, arid valleys of northern Afghanistan until it finally unrolls on the flat steppe at the southern edge of Central Asia. The interpreter thought back to the year before when he and Corinne had taken the same road to Mazar and back. Doing Shakespeare in Kabul was then an idea yet unformed. So much had happened since.

The interpreter sat in the front seat of one of the vans enjoying the magnificent landscape. At a place north of Salang, he looked across a broad river valley at the ruins of a town the Soviets had obliterated some twenty years before. It was one of the many places they had "carpet bombed" to punish those opposed to their rule. He could see the walls of one or two ruined buildings still partially standing, and little else. So many of Afghanistan's present troubles, he mused, had roots in the Soviet occupation.

Shah Mohammed was wedged between the interpreter and the driver. The actors were exuberant people. They loved to sing, and laugh, and be mad at someone. They all needed to talk, often all at the same time. When they stopped for rest breaks, they all wanted to change vans, and did so several times. In his role as tour manager, the interpreter had to run from van to van to make sure everyone was back in the vehicles before they started driving again, and not wandering along the river, or behind a rock answering the call of nature.

The driver of his van was named Rahman. He could sing better and louder than the actors, which he did while speeding up and down the switch-back mountain roads. Everyone wanted to be in Rahman's van. Nabi sat in the back, drumming the *tabla*, while Shah Mohammed in the front accompanied Rahman on the harmonium. The rest clapped from wherever they sat, led by Kabir. Rahman had a rough voice, probably because he smoked non-stop, even while he was singing. Every time he lit a cigarette, he kept one between his lips, and gave others to the actors in the back seat. After every song, Nabi would shout out, "Oh, long life, Rahman, long life!" and Rahman would reply, "Nabi jan, Let's play another song."

At one point in the mountains, Nabi took off his T-shirt, popped his head through an opening in the van's roof, though the air was freezing cold, and shouted, "This clean air is pure medicine. Inhale! Inhale to the bottom of your lungs, to the core of your heart, to the depths of your intestines!"

Everyone else was shivering in the van and shouted at him to close the roof, but Nabi was relishing his encounter with nature. He stayed aloft with his arms outspread as if he were Kate Winslet on the prow of the *Titanic*. Finally, he sat down and closed the roof, though only after the others begged him to sing another song.

:::::

They reached Mazar around 4:00 PM. The Foundation had booked lodgings for them at the Hotel Mazar. There were many good hotels in Mazar, but the Hotel Mazar was not one of them.

"None of the rooms have a bathroom," Shah Mohammed said with a puzzled look. "Are we supposed to use the communal toilets? They are one floor below and they smell awful." Indeed, it turned out that everyone else in the hotel was expected to share them as well.

Then the girls discovered that there was no hot water.

Breshna held out her hair from under her headscarf. "How are we going to shampoo in cold water?" she asked the interpreter.

The rooms were dirty, the old metal beds squeaked, the mattresses were stained and hard, the pillows and sheets were soiled, and layers of dust covered everything.

The interpreter became anxious. The Foundation's office in Mazar had assured Robert that "everything has been organized." Looking at the kind of lodgings they had arranged, he wondered. He decided he had best go and check with them on everything else.

By the time he reached the Foundation's small office near the center of Mazar, all of the staff had gone home for the day, except for the director. After the usual pleasantries and drinking a glass of tea, the interpreter asked if everything were ready. The director looked surprised. "Ready for what?" he asked.

"For the play," the interpreter replied pleasantly. "The chairs, the tent, the security, the tea or water for the audience, the invitation cards, everything. In fact, where is the show going to be held?"

"What is the rush for?" He looked at the interpreter as if he were crazy. "The show is next week."

"No, it is the day after tomorrow."

"What?" The director showed the interpreter the printed invitation cards that were dated for the following week. No one in Kabul had told him that, with the cancellation of the show in Herat, the actors were coming to Mazar a week earlier than originally planned.

⁛⁛⁛

The next day, everything had to be done. The brochures that had been printed with what was now the wrong date could not be used. The interpreter asked the director to get someone with a loudspeaker in a truck to announce the performance for the next day. Then he went to a place that rented chairs for weddings and made a deal to have a couple of hundred delivered the following morning to Azadi Park in front of the Governor's Residence, where the performance would be held.

Like most parks in Afghanistan, Azadi Park had some tall pine trees, but no grass. Thick, powdery dust covered the feet of anyone who walked there. Some cheap carpets would have to be rented to create a place for the actors to perform. Otherwise, they would choke when they tried to speak.

Then the interpreter went to the mayor, Atta Mohammed, to tell him what was being arranged, and to request that he provide security the next day. He had to wait half an hour for the mayor to finish a meeting with some sportsmen who had just returned home from an international competition wearing medals.

The mayor told the interpreter to talk to the chief of police, then called the chief on his mobile, instructing him to help. At the police department, the interpreter drank tea for nearly an hour while waiting for the chief to arrive. When he did, he was polite, but asked endless questions about the play: why was it being done; was there anything touchy in the show; why Shakespeare, and why not an Afghan play; which actors were in the play; what kind of security did he want; who was directing the play; why was the director not there; was the interpreter making excuses for her because there was something touchy in the play that might reflect badly on her; and so on and so on.

This discussion went on for nearly an hour before the chief of police gave his permission for the show to be performed, and started making security arrangements.

::·:·:·

Having no obligations that afternoon, the actors had decided to go to the blue-tiled shrine of Hazrat Ali. Any Afghan coming to Mazar would feel compelled to pray there, and to walk through its gardens filled with roses and white doves.

The serenity that normally surrounds the shrine, however, was soon seriously disturbed.

Rahman saw what happened and described it later to the interpreter. He had dropped off the actors at the gate to the shrine's gardens, and had gone to park the van in a shady spot. Shortly after, when he stepped out to buy an orange from a street vendor, he noticed a large crowd gathering inside the gardens. He kept straining his eyes in the glaring sunlight, trying to see what was going on. Breshna Bahar and the girls had been heading to find the Jogee women, who sit on the sidewalks with their babies tied to their backs, selling glass bracelets of many colors. Part of the great tribe known elsewhere as Roma, the Jogee women peddle trinkets and beg from the pilgrims. Those seeking divine favor may feel that their chances are improved by showing a little generosity themselves.

Rahman scanned the rows of Jogee women to see if he could spot Breshna.

"Suddenly," Rahman said, "I realized that it was Nabi and Breshna in the middle of the crowd. A mob of people were standing all around them, and shouting 'Bulbul! Bulbul!' There were so many people that they could hardly move."

They managed to get into the shrine to do their prayers, but by the time they had come out, even more people had gathered, all wanting to get Nabi's and Breshna's autographs. Breshna and Nabi had to fight their way back to the van, and then Rahman rushed them to the hotel to try to escape all their fans. But many of them ran after the van.

"I think the word has spread and now everybody in Mazar seems to be standing outside the hotel hoping to get a glimpse of them," Rahman said. "The security came out to disperse them, but they would not leave."

The interpreter had had to push his way through the crowd when he returned to the hotel. Mostly it was young men in *shalwar kameez*, with a number of police standing nearby with sticks in their hands. They all seemed to be smiling, even the police.

"I was terrified," Breshna said later. "I really felt trapped by the crowd." Though she had stared down many vicious criminals in her police work, she said that nothing she had experienced as a policewoman had felt as frightening. The interpreter had to go and buy *burqas* for her and the other girls so they could leave the hotel unnoticed. Nabi was forced to stay inside. He shouted at the interpreter as he often had at Corinne. The interpreter smiled at him, and gave him a big hug. Nabi untangled himself and walked away.

Nabi sat in his hotel room, clearly shaken. He was nervous about what sort of crowd would come to the performance the next afternoon.

"We have to be concerned about the reaction of the audience," Nabi said, "because you never know who they are – educated people or fundamentalists. Even if we have only one fundamentalist in the audience, it takes only one bomb to blow everybody up."

Might there be a bomber among them? No one knew. Was there really any way to protect the actors on the stage? No one could say.

:::::

The next day the interpreter went to Azadi Park early. The chairs arrived late, the carpets arrived late. No one came with the chairs to set them up in rows, or with the carpets to arrange them on the ground to make a performance area. Mustafa was not there to help. The interpreter had to set the whole place up himself with a few passersby whom he asked to help. There was no tent where the actors could put on their costumes. They had to dress in the hotel, and come to the park ready to perform.

Two hours before the show, the park started filling up with people. Every plastic chair was full, with at least two people on every seat. Some cracked. Some broke. There were at least three hundred chairs. Hundreds of other spectators were standing behind them, probably more than a thousand in all, with still more in the trees. Most were workmen and people from the street who had heard the loudspeaker truck. They did not know what a play was. They just knew that Nabi and Breshna would be there. Soldiers perched to get a good view on nearby army tanks, sent by the police chief along with several dozen policemen carrying Kalashnikovs.

A short while before the actors arrived, the weather grew windy and dust spun in small funnels through the park. Some men sprinkled water on the ground around the performance area to damp down the dust. The security officers sent by the chief of police showed up, distracting the interpreter with a stream of questions. They appeared to be less interested in controlling the crowd than in seeing Bulbul and Gul Chera, and having their pictures taken with them. The interpreter was feeling exhausted. He had been running like a dog since morning and not had any lunch. He had to be nice to the security men, though, and answer all their questions. They had guns.

As the crowd was filling the park, two women in *burqas* arrived and sat in chairs near the front, to one side. They were the only women there, apart from the actresses. Just before the show began, however, a man came and, without speaking to them, led them away. They made no attempt to argue, and but left quietly, the security men giving them a hand to climb a high step that led out of the park.

Finally, the show started. No one could hear what the actors were saying in the first scene in which only the men appeared, because so many in the audience kept shouting, "Bulbul, where is Gul Chera?" And when Breshna finally appeared, they yelled even louder.

The actors performed all their scenes as they had rehearsed them, even though no one in the crowd seemed to understand Shakespeare's poetry. For such an audience, something very simple would have worked better. Of course, the audience, which kept growing, loved the Indian scene the most. Some danced along with the actors.

As the performance proceeded, the actors began to relax. The crowd was huge, but it felt friendly. It became apparent that if someone were going to set off a bomb or interfere with the actors, they would have to deal with everyone else as well. Still, the boys had decided to take the precaution of wearing T-shirts with their *dhotis*, not certain whether local sensibilities might be offended by seeing bare-chested men in public.

At the end of the play, some of the audience rushed the stage to ask the actors for their autographs, especially Bulbul and Gul Chera. They were so many that the security officers could not hold them back. Things quickly got out of control. With the help of a few Afghan soldiers, the actors were pushed one by one into the vans, and the drivers were told to go as fast as they could back to the hotel.

The crowd was so thick, though, that at first the vehicles could barely inch along. Rahman blasted his horn a couple of times, but that only made the crowd cheer. Then, slowly, they opened a path so the vans could move. Nabi sat in the front seat looking like a very important man, smiling and waving to the crowd, and shaking some hands through the open window.

::::::

The next morning the actors were scheduled to perform at a girl's school. When they arrived, though, they discovered that the news had preceded them that Bulbul and Gul Chera were on their way. The actors in their costumes looked as if they were going to a very fancy wedding party. The students, in their black school outfits and white head scarves, whispered loudly to their friends when they finally saw Nabi and Breshna, Within moments, they were shrieking. And, like a volcano, they erupted out of their classrooms and rushed into the schoolyard. Their teachers could do nothing to restrain them.

The students surrounded the actors for several minutes until the teachers started issuing orders for them to sit on the ground. No one could stop the shrieking. The boys prepared to start the play. The girls stood to one side waiting for their cue. The boys began the first scene. No one could hear what they were saying. The students were too excited to listen. The boys continued as best they could until the scene called for them to sing a song. Suddenly the students quieted.

By then the actors understood that doing a full performance there was probably not going to be possible that day. So, instead, the girls joined the boys on stage. Together they sang all the songs in the play, along with a couple of others. The students were thrilled, and cheered loudly when, after half an hour, the actors stood up to leave. Perhaps they had not experienced Shakespeare, but they had encountered the power of a live performance.

Herat

Herat. May 2006.

Within a week of returning from Mazar, the interpreter received a call from the Governor of Herat. He had decided to allow the actors to do a show there after all, but only as a private performance within the walls of the Citadel to an audience who would be there by invitation. Any hopes of doing the play in a public park or in schools were quashed.

The actors took an afternoon plane to Herat, as Corinne again remained in Kabul. They mounted the stairs to the plane, waving like celebrities to Nabi on the tarmac who was videotaping everything. Faisal sported a necktie and, uncharacteristically, was clean shaven. He looked like a businessman heading to a conference. For a few of the actors, it was their first time flying. They examined the safety cards with interest and asked the flight attendants many questions, then they kept their faces glued to the windows as the plane took off and lifted over the dusty, familiar streets of Kabul.

The actors had been booked into the faded, once-elegant Mawfaq Hotel. The swimming pool had weeds growing through its cracks, but the rooms were marginally better than those in Mazar. By now, the actors knew what to expect when touring. At least they had water, most of the time. The staff was run ragged bringing tea to the actors' rooms and responding to their endless requests. They did not seem to mind since Bulbul and Gul Chera were the most demanding, and they were famous.

Nabi and Breshna stayed in the hotel, not wanting to risk repeating the mob scenes of Mazar. The others wandered off in twos and threes through Herat, enjoying the air that was far cleaner than in Kabul. There were traffic lights, then unknown in Kabul, and, to everyone's surprise, the drivers actually obeyed them. Sidewalk bazaars sold everything from women's undergarments to switchblades. A long park ran in front of the hotel. It was filled with flowers and people sitting on the grass. Many of them sipped tea provided by push-cart vendors.

Some of the actors and the interpreter walked into the old part of the city near the vast Jumaa Mosque, which had been built in 1200. Its immense portal and towering minarets were covered in ceramic tiles in deep shades of blue, yellow, pink and green, creating dazzling multicolored patterns. The mosque's courtyard could hold more than a thousand worshippers. Its marble paving stones burned everyone's bare feet until a young man suggested they walk only on the white marble. He was right. The white was much cooler. They were grateful, and invited him to the play the next day.

:::::

From the Jumaa Mosque, they walked the short distance to the Citadel. The interpreter wanted to make sure that everything was ready, with none of the surprises they had encountered in Mazar.

Jolyon Leslie and his team from the Aga Khan Trust for Culture were in the midst of a reconstruction of the Citadel that would take several years, similar to what they were doing at the Bagh-e Babur in Kabul. They had offered to provide chairs, security and anything else the actors needed.

Arash Boostani, an Iranian engineer overseeing the restoration, had indeed arranged everything. He served tea in a low workshop building in front of the massive walls that had been under construction when Alexander of Macedon had arrived in 330 BCE. He unrolled large plans of the Citadel, indicating which parts had already been reconstructed and which they would be working on next.

Then he led the group through a huge gate, and up to an inner fort that sits at the highest point of the Citadel like an eagles nest over Herat. In one direction, they could see the Jumaa Mosque where it rose up out of the Old City, whose neat grid-like streets stretched below. In the other, they had a clear view of the remnants of a palace and madrasa complex built in the early 1400s by Tamburlaine's son, Shah Rukh, and his wife, Gowhar Shad. Together, they had fostered a golden age for the arts in Herat. Gravity-defying minarets leaned in all directions, held erect now by cables. Beyond the minarets were the mountains.

Arash explained that there had been many more minarets, but a century ago British military commanders ordered them destroyed, claiming they could be used as cover by the Russians if they ever attacked Herat. The attack never came. Most of the minarets lie in ruins. This is the sad story of Afghan history.

∴∴∴∴

When the actors got back to the Mawfaq Hotel, no one was there except Parwin. The others, she said, had gone to the candy market to buy some sweets and pastries. Anyone who goes to Mazar feels obligated to visit the shrine. In Herat, they have to go to the candy market. About half an hour later, Faisal and Aref arrived with bags filled with all kinds of sweets. By then it was dark.

With the show the next day, the plan was to have an early meal and a quiet evening. Nabi and Shah Mohammed did not go out with the others. Nabi had had a fight with Breshna that afternoon and refused to eat with her. Shah Mohammed did what Nabi did. Of course, the next day they had forgotten whatever had so vexed them the night before and everything was placid between them.

The rest of the actors went to the Arghawan Restaurant and sat on raised platforms built in alcoves around a rock-pile fountain full of frolicking cement deer, but no water. A painting of Maryam, the mother of Prophet Issa [Jesus], hung on one wall. The waiter who served them was very excited to see the actors.

Later, they all went out to the park that stretched down the centre of the main boulevard along the north side of the Old City. From it, they could see portions of the thousand-year-old city walls a short distance away. They found some water pipe vendors in the park, and settled in for a relaxing hour of sucking in apple-scented tobacco smoke. The interpreter laughed to himself that in a city with clean air, everyone wanted to breathe smoke.

For the actors, freed from their obligations at home, this was as close to a vacation as some of them had ever experienced. The concept of "leisure time" is all but unknown in Afghanistan. The pleasing atmosphere of Herat put everyone in a good mood. Even their cosmic complaints were gentled. The most anyone could find to moan about was the wind. While it is true that every year Herat has one hundred or more days of wind, that night there was hardly a breeze. The soft air caressed everyone's faces, and carried the blue smoke from the pipes to search for the noses of people happy to smell it.

:::::

The next day, the actors were not pleased with the breakfast that the hotel served. Money was collected and given to Aref and Nazeef to go buy the best food they could find. They brought back a feast of chicken and lamb kebab and *qabuli pelau*. Soon, the complaints were replaced by jokes and singing.

There were still several hours before the performance, so some of the actors who had not visited the Citadel the day before decided to go and take a look at it. Like many historic buildings, it had been closed to the public for at least twenty years.

As soon as they got inside its gates, they started running around like kids who had been brought to a marvelous playground. They climbed up one tower, then the next. From the top, they took photos of beautiful views of Herat spread below. They were truly amazed by the size of the Citadel, by its elegantly constructed arches and its high walls. Wajma said it looked as if it had been built by giants. They started telling each other heroic tales.

Leila struck a pose in front of a towering column and proclaimed, "There was a queen here. She was the ruler of this place. She had thousands at her disposal, all of them her servants. She used to sit on a chair made of gold and covered with diamonds. With the flick of a finger, her orders were fulfilled. People feared and loved her. They feared her because she could do anything, and loved her because she was mighty and kind to her people. When she went out, she traveled in splendid style in a horse-drawn carriage escorted by bodyguards of cavalry."

Faisal raised his arms in protest, as if shocked by her pronouncements. "No, it was a man who ruled this place. He had thousands of soldiers waiting for his orders. He was exalted throughout the region. Every boy dreamed of being like him one day. He was a legend, the greatest conqueror the world has ever known. He had a ferocious army that blazed across the world, razing cites, torturing and decapitating his enemies. He had poets, philosophers, thinkers, writers, storytellers, musicians, and clowns waiting for him to clap his hands and tell them, 'Come.'"

People like that really had lived in this place. Perhaps Leila and Faisal were hearing the whispers of their ghosts, the interpreter wondered.

As the day grew warmer, the actors grew tired of exploring. The sun was intense, and the wind was a real wind now, not just a breeze. Nabi suggested that they should go through the script to pass the time. They went inside some rooms in the Citadel that they would be using as dressing rooms. With its mud-brick walls and domes, they were pleasantly cool.

The actors sat on the floor in a circle, and started reciting their lines. They put their texts on the ground. No one made mistakes. No one was nervous or unhappy. Everyone was comfortable with one another. When they had finished, Nabi looked at everyone. "Last year, we performed in the Foundation and Babur's garden, and we had no one looking after our security. There were no guns to be seen," he said. "Now we perform in a Citadel, and the Governor is sending police to keep us safe. What is happening to this country all over again? Why can't life be as smooth and easy as it is for so many other countries?"

No one said anything, because no one had answers to Nabi's questions.

:::::

Around 4:00 PM, the audience started to arrive, about two hundred and fifty of them in all. A large number of women from Herat University came as a group. They seemed to float as they walked, draped in pleated blue *burqas*. Once inside the Citadel's second set of walls, however, the women pulled off the *burqas* and became chattering young women, many in designer jeans. The *burqas* were folded and placed carefully over the backs of their chairs as they settled down to watch the play. Many young men, also from the university, joined them. Most wore stylish Western clothes.

The show went smoothly. A few Afghan soldiers who had been appointed to provide security inside the Citadel were so caught up in the play that they came and stood near the platform when the actors did their first scene, and stayed there transfixed until the end of the play. They were probably uneducated, and maybe even illiterate, but Shakespeare's poetry kept them rapt.

The real star of the show was the Citadel. *Love's Labour's Lost* takes place in front of a castle. The Foundation for Culture and Civil Society had provided a beautiful garden and a palatial house, but it was not a castle. The Bagh-e Babur had stone battlements that looked like a castle, but, in fact, were not one. The Citadel of Herat, the Qala Ikhtyaruddin, truly was a castle. Line upon line of yellow brick arches rose behind the stage. In every direction, high stone towers dominated the view. Walls surrounded the performance space, and a moat encompassed them. As the play progressed and the sun dipped, the yellow brick walls turned to a fiery gold.

The audience listened carefully to every word. Many of them were studying literature. Most said that this was the first play they had ever seen. At the first jokes, they smiled, and looked at one another. They were not sure if they were allowed to laugh. When the girls entered in their brightly-colored costumes, many of the women sat up straighter to get a better view. The jokes began to get bigger laughs. By the time the boys had revealed to each other that they had all fallen in love, the audience had lost its inhibitions. Then came the scene with the Indian songs, and – as was now fully expected – they all went crazy. As they had in Mazar, all the boys but Shah Mohammed chose to wear their black T-shirts with their dhotis.

Not one thing went wrong in that show. It was the last performance of *Love's Labour's Lost*, and was probably the best the actors had ever given.

⁞⁞⁞⁞

As was now customary, members of the audience gathered around the actors after the show as if trying to extend the good feelings it had created. Everyone was excited, but especially the women in the audience. One of them thanked Breshna and the other women in the cast profusely, saying, "This is the first time a woman has been on stage in Herat. Now more will follow, because it won't be taboo anymore."

Two weeks later, a bomb went off at Herat University, protesting the education of women. Four young women were killed. The actors could only wonder if any of those who had come to see the play were among the dead.

⁞⁞⁞⁞

When the actors had finished speaking with some Herati journalists who had come to interview them, they went to the domed dressing room, where cakes and cookies had been arranged for them. Nabi poured tea into a plastic cup and sipped some. He spat it out and said, "This tea smells like burning plastic."

"It is not the tea," Shah Mohammed explained, "It is the plastic tea cups that make it smell like that."

"Aga Khan's wealth is all over the world," Nabi railed, "yet he serves us tea in plastic." He put his cup on the table. By now everyone knew that when Nabi was fussing, he was happy. They watched him as he ate some cake and cookies, talked to the actors, and absent-mindedly picked up his cup again and took a sip. He forcefully spat the hot liquid back into the cup, saying, "Why do I keep reaching for this smelly plastic tea?"

"Because you are thirsty," Shah Mohammed stated with mock solicitude. Everyone laughed except Nabi.

"Find me some water," Nabi ordered imperiously to no one in particular, and no one paid any attention to him.

There were parts of *Love's Labour's Lost* that the interpreter would miss. And parts that he would not.

::::::

That night none of the actors fought or argued with each other. That should have put everyone on notice that somebody would soon start something.

They all returned to the restaurant they had visited the night before, the Arghawan, to enjoy its good food, and to laugh at its dry fountain with the cement deer. Later they went again to smoke water pipes in the park. And then, quite unexpectedly, a *shehr jangi*, a poetry battle, started.

It began when Nabi blew a huge puff of smoke into the darkening sky and recited one of his most poetic speeches from *Love's Labour's Lost*. Perhaps he was expecting applause. Instead, Leila responded by reciting a sonnet by Rumi in a competitive tone. Her selection started with the last letter of Nabi's poem, which was a loud and clear message that she was challenging him to come back with something better.

Nabi's faithful lieutenant Shah Mohammed stepped in and recited a two-verse poem that started with the last letter of Leila's poem. Now, if anyone had doubted it, they were having an all-out battle, and the boys were pitted against the girls.

Quickly, the stakes were raised. It was no longer good enough just to recite a poem that started with the last letter of the previous one. If one of the boys recited a two- or four-verse poem about love, one of the girls had to reply with a poem about the deeper meaning of love, devotion or being loyal. And so it went, shifting from love poems to spiritual poems, to epic poems, to patriotic poems, back to love poems, and so on.

Aref, for example, recited a couplet by Hafez against the girls, while he looked all of them in the eye:

O beloved, I promise I will never turn my face away from you again,
Even if you stone me, or with curses drive me away.

Leila jumped in with a couplet by the same poet that started with the Dari equivalent of the letter "Y":

You are the messenger of the mystery, and now
I know I'm on the right path,
So, do not give me orders, but urge me gently on.

Everyone cheered, "Bravo, Leila jan!"

Faisal then joined the fight and recited a couplet against Leila and all the girls with a poem that started with the letter "N":

Not even a hundred beautiful women could lure me from this place,
Could ambush my heart with an army of idols reeking of perfume.

The boys shouted, "Bravo, Faisal jan!"

Breshna then took it upon herself to avenge the girls. She recited a four-verse poem from Rumi against Faisal and all the boys. It started with the letter "E":

Eternity waits behind the transparent door
Of each moment. Love the beloved, and that door
Swings open: Eternity enters, pouring the wine
No one who drinks can ever recover from.

All the girls yelled, "Breshna jan!"

Now the contest was slowly shifting to spiritual poems. One of the boys had to do a poem starting with the letter "M", but not about love, but rather about something deeper. Nabi recited:

My heart has run on water all day,
And will pray on Sinai all night,
Yet some say, "No one can walk on water,
Or climb up Sinai without feet."

All the boys cheered.

Up until then, Parwin had been quietly listening, silent except for bursts of her melodic laughter. Unexpectedly, she began to recite:

They prattle of "balance," of "moderation," of "decorum,"
I wrote on one of the doors in secret:
"You think you know, you died long ago;
You think you see? Reason ate your eyes."

The girls clapped and said, "Excellent, Parwin jan!" The boys looked at one another for several moments, but no one could come up with something as strong as Parwin had just recited, even though they all had poems they could give that started with the letter "S." Parwin's poem had been a heavyweight, and none of the boys could find one its equal. When the pause lasted for more than half a minute, first one of the girls, then all of them, started shouting: "We won!" They had indeed.

Gloomy looks swept over the boys' faces. They had fought hard, but had been tripped up by the soft-spoken Parwin. They demanded a rematch. The interpreter had to start it with a new poem, and it did not matter what it was about. He chose his favorite verses by Maulana Jala-e-Din Mohammed Balkhi, known to the world as Rumi:

Come, come, whoever you are, wanderer, worshiper, lover of leaving:
It doesn't matter –
Ours is not a caravan of despair,
but one of endless joy.
Even if you have broken your vows a hundred times –
Come, come, yet again, come!

And with those sweet words of spiritual invitation and ecstasy, the battle commenced anew.

By then it was past midnight, but the competition continued for another three and a half hours. All of the boys and the girls were sleepy, but no one wanted to stop as long as the other side was winning. They finally called a truce, with the score tied.

The interpreter was happy and proud. The poetry contest had kept the actors busy, and given them no chance to complain to him about anything. He realized that if they had kept copies of all the poems they had recited in the competition, from beginning to end, their poems would have made a very thick book. These people could drive him crazy sometimes, but he was grateful that *Love's Labour's Lost* had allowed him to get to know them.

:::::

Everyone went to the hotel to catch a few hours of sleep. That did not mean, however, that the contest ended there. It continued the next day as soon as everyone woke up, erupting again while they were having breakfast. A few of the waiters joined in as they served *naan*, yoghurt and tea. No one won.

Again a truce was called as they packed their bags and went to the airport. In the terminal, it started again. A few passengers offered poems. Still no one won. The contest did not stop in the plane; it continued at 30,000 feet, as two of the flight attendants participated. No one won.

They reached Kabul at the end of the day, and it continued all the way to the baggage claim. A man who had arrived from Kandahar a few minutes ahead of their flight joined in with the actors as he waited for his luggage. He was fast, and his poems were sharp. Unfortunately, though, every poem he recited, the actors had already heard. He had no way of knowing that the contest was by then nearly seventeen hours old with no repeats. The actors made fun of him for reciting verses they had already used. He offered one poem after another, more than ten of them. No sooner had he recited the opening verse, than the actors in one loud voice exclaimed mockingly, "Old one!"

He laughed, and said, "You people are way too far ahead of me. Goodbye!" He put the strap of his bag on his shoulder and stepped to one side as the baggage belt began moving.

Shah Mohammed quickly recited a poem to jab him for not being able to compete:

The beauty of this poem is beyond words.
Do you need a guide to experience the heat of the sun?

Everyone laughed, including the man from Kandahar. "Good one!" he said, as he waited for his bags to arrive.

Shy Kabir suddenly recited another poem to poke more fun at him:

If you wake up tomorrow with headache or hangover,
Drink more wine, and chase this discomfort away.

The man smiled slightly. Everyone could see that he was no longer enjoying this. Then Aref lobbed another one, which made everyone roar with laughter, except for the man, who was becoming embarrassed. It had stopped being a joke for him. Aref recited:

O fool, do something, so you won't just stand there looking dumb.
If you are not traveling and on the road, how can you call yourself a
guide?

The baggage arrived. The Kandahari man grabbed his, and quickly disappeared.

As soon as the actors were out of the terminal, the contest started again. Daoud had come to the airport to pick them up. When he saw what was going on, he joined in. Soon he realized the actors were way ahead of him. He started reciting poems in Pashto, and brought a new level of complexity to the contest, which made everyone happier. When he dropped the girls off at their homes, they said their goodbyes with poems. The contest continued. No one won.

:::::

The next day all the actors met at the Foundation. The battle began afresh. Corinne wanted to hear all the details of the performance in Herat. When she asked the actors about the show, they answered by pelting poems at the other side. Corinne wanted to know what was being said. The interpreter explained to her that it was a poetry contest, that it had been going on since two nights before, and that it was not easy to translate the verses. They were coming too fast. In the end, the interpreter appointed himself the judge and announced that both parties were equal. No one won.

Everyone was upset by that. In Afghanistan, the only thing worse than losing is ending in a tie. They complained loudly, but they know that a judge can do anything he wants.

In truth, it was better for both parties not to have the other the clear winner. If the boys were declared the winners, the girls would only want to challenge them again. And if the girls had won, the boys would be forced to challenge them. It was a question of honor. And it could go on like that for days.

∴∴∴

And that is how their production of *Love's Labour's Lost* ended: on a wave of sublime poetry and fierce competition.

Ten Years After

Ten Years After

2015

Love's Labour's Lost had ended, but for the actors their journey into an uncertain future had just begun.

Within a year, Nabi Tanha was cast in the Hollywood film of Khaled Hosseini's novel, *The Kite Runner*. His scenes were shot in Kashgar in western China, which looked more like the Kabul of Hosseini's youth than the war-scarred city that Kabul had become. Nabi was away for a summer. After he returned to Kabul, he rarely performed again. He focused instead on producing commercials for television.

Aref Bahunar was invited by French theater director Ariane Mnouchkine to study in Paris as a member of the Aftaab Theater, a company she set up to train Afghan actors. With Aftaab, Aref performed many plays in France and toured around Spain and Italy. Paris eventually became his home, though he has a daughter and a son "whom I love more than anything in the world. But every minute of the day I suffer because I can't easily see them. They are in Kabul and I'm in Paris. Hopefully, we will be united one day in our country where I can teach the new generation about theater and acting, everything I learned here."

Saba Sahar continued writing, directing and producing successful films and television series, but at a cost. Her husband's family objected to her acting, which put stresses on their marriage. She remained deeply committed to her work, however, both in championing the rule of law to resolve Afghanistan's social problems, and in encouraging young women to follow her into careers in police work and film-making. She told a British journalist in 2012, "I have two messages for Afghan women and girls. First they should never think they are weak, second they must have self-confidence."

:::::

Corinne returned to Kabul the next three summers to direct a much smaller theater project. It was called *Sisters* and was only for the girls. It was based on stories from their own lives. Breshna Bahar and her daughter Wajma were among the cast, as were Parwin Mushtahel, Marina Golbahari and Leila.

In 2009, Ariane Mnouchkine invited them to perform *Sisters* in Paris at her Cartoucherie theater complex. During the six weeks that the girls spent there, living in quaint 19th-century horse-drawn caravans amid the lush greenery of the Bois de Vincennes, they made a startling discovery: they were all desperately homesick for dusty Kabul, especially for the food and the *naan*.

:::::

As the girls were preparing to take the show to Paris in 2009, a terrible thing happened to Parwin and her husband, Tawab.

After Tawab and Parwin had been forced to leave her sister's house during *Love's Labour's Lost*, they had lived for several months with Breshna, who had immediately offered them shelter when she heard what had happened. Eventually, Tawab and Parwin bought a piece of land in a neighborhood called Tepe-e Bala Hissar, near a large cemetery. They did not know anyone in the area. Occasionally, Parwin heard rude remarks from people in the area who recognized her from something she had done on television. She ignored them, but grew uneasy when Tawab started receiving mysterious phone calls. When he asked who it was, there was no answer.

Finally one day the caller spoke and demanded that Parwin stop acting. It was a man speaking in Pashto.

One evening, someone knocked loudly on the door. When Tawab went to see who it was, no one was there. A short time later, though, the knocking started again. This time they could hear someone yelling as well. They ignored him. The next evening at around five o'clock, the knocking started again and they heard the same voice from the night before shouting in Pashto for Tawab to come out and meet him.

"Though it was getting dark, my husband said it would be better if he went to talk to him," Parwin recounted afterwards. "Tawab did not come back right away, as I had expected. In fact, after one hour, he had still not come back. By then it was completely dark, and we had no electricity for lights. I was becoming very scared. I called him several times, but his phone was turned off."

At eight o'clock, she heard three shots. She started to shake. She was too frightened to scream.

"I couldn't go out," said Parwin. "I was alone with my children, and there was no other man in my family. We had no relatives nearby. I didn't even know my neighbors well, so I couldn't call and ask anybody what was going on. I could feel that something had happened, but I didn't know what. My children started crying, and asking where their dad was. I just said that he would come. I locked the door of the house, and stayed awake all night. I was afraid that someone might come for me and the children."

In the morning, she could hear other voices in the street. Through her window, she saw a policeman come through her gate, and walk across the garden toward the house. She started to pray as she opened the door to him.

He addressed her formally in a quiet voice. "*Hamshira*," – which means "sister" – "I must tell you something, but my mouth does not wish to make these words." Parwin could hold back the tears no longer. Her daughter and son started to cry as well, not knowing what was happening.

A neighbor's wife and sister came running into the house,

wailing and screaming and praying loudly. Outside, across the street from the house at the edge of the cemetery, Tawab lay dead, the blood from a gaping wound in his face now dried in the dust. His body had been mutilated.

Parwin and her children fled from the house that same day. She and her husband had tried so hard not to upset anyone with her work. They thought they could outrun the gossip. She went to her sister's house for that night, and then to a different house the next night, and to still a different house the night after. Her husband's eight brothers took Tawab's body to Khost for burial, and organized the funeral there.

Parwin never saw Tawab again, nor had a chance to say goodbye. She put on a *burqa* so no one would recognize her on the street. She went to the police, and even to the Minister of Interior Affairs asking for justice. No one listened to her. The indescribable grief that wracked her was made even worse by her disappointment in the new government that once had promised so much.

"Don't look too deep. The other party is very dangerous." A policeman cornered her as she walked out of the police station. "All you are doing is digging your own grave. If I were you, I would shut my mouth and disappear. Your husband is the victim of your art. Instead of you, he paid the price."

In the weeks that followed, Parwin and the children fled to Pakistan, where they thought they would be safe. Just before leaving, she called the interpreter and told him between fits of crying all that had happened. The interpreter sent an email to Corinne and others who knew Parwin. Corinne in Paris went into overdrive, seeking assistance from the UN High Commission for Refugees, and from the French and Canadian Embassies in Pakistan. She made phone calls and sent e-mails by the dozen. She was relentless in her efforts.

She was helped by a Canadian theater director, Christopher Morris, who had been in Kabul some months earlier looking for an Afghan actress for a play he was planning to direct at his Human Cargo Theater in Toronto. He had met Parwin, and was deeply moved when he had heard about the pressure she was then under from her family. Now he was utterly horrified by what had happened. He worked as tirelessly as Corinne to get Parwin out of danger.

Months of e-mails, phone calls and pleas to bureaucrats and diplomats followed. Christina Lamb, a journalist from *The Sunday Times* in London who had published a much-acclaimed book about Afghanistan, *The Sewing Circles of Herat*, wrote a feature story about Parwin that captured the agony that she and her children were enduring.

For months, Parwin stayed in her house, terrified every time she had to go out, even to buy food. Her thoughts rambled from one thing to the next. She thought about her parents: her father, a poet, had been the head of landscape design for the Ministry of Public Affairs, and her mother a literature teacher at Zarghona High School. They were good people who had educated their six daughters. Yet they had suffered the loss of three sons; the oldest, also a poet, died during the Russian invasion of Afghanistan; the second during the years of civil war; and the third during the American invasion of Afghanistan, when shrapnel of a bomb hit him. "Why so much sorrow for one family?" Parwin asked herself over and over.

She had been married to Tawab for eleven years. After the Taliban had taken over, they had moved to rural Khost to live with his extended family. They thought it would be safer in his family's village. There she was known among the adults as Dr. Parwin, because she could give them notes to take to a pharmacy for simple medications for headache, joint pains, coughs and other basic sicknesses. They allowed her to teach the boys and girls how to read and write. After she and Tawab moved back to Kabul to make it easier for him to travel to Dubai, Pakistan and Tajikistan to buy cars and spare parts for his business, Parwin held secret classes in her home for girls until she was discovered by the Taliban. She stopped teaching and lived in hiding for a few months. Now she was hiding again. What crime had she committed that she must always be fleeing to the shadows?

One day, two men whom Parwin did not recognize showed up at the house in Islamabad. They threatened her and the children. Again she fled, first to a mosque, and then to a women's shelter.

It took a year of unyielding efforts by Corinne in Paris and Christopher Morris in Canada before Parwin and the kids were finally given UN refugee documents and entry visas to Canada.

Parwin, Shogufa and Ahmad landed in Toronto exhausted and terrified, but eagerly welcomed by the group of Canadians whom Christopher Morris had gathered to help them get resettled. Six months later, the children were speaking English, and Parwin was beginning not to panic when she heard a knock at the door.

∵∵∵

In late 2010, Corinne was contacted by Shakespeare's Globe Theater in London and asked if she might direct her *Love's Labour's Lost* troupe in a different play in May 2012. The Globe was planning to present all of Shakespeare's plays in languages other than English to coincide with the London Olympics that year. They proposed *Richard II*.

"Afghans don't do tragedy," Corinne told them.

"*The Comedy of Errors?*" they asked.

"Let's talk," she replied.

The British Council in Kabul again offered financial support, as well as the use of their recently-opened center in Kabul. Corinne went to Kabul in August 2011 to start looking for the six men and three women she needed for the cast.

The interpreter called all the actors from *Love's Labour's Lost* and told them to get ready for another Shakespeare journey. He also contacted many new actors who were becoming known in Kabul as well as many women who had started working as actresses. By then, there was no lack of actresses in Kabul. For a week, Corinne and the interpreter auditioned more than five of them every day.

On August 19, 2011, the British Council compound was attacked just before dawn; twelve people were killed. Corinne, the interpreter and the actors were not there that day. It was a Friday, the Muslim holy day. She had had no plans to meet them or be there. Nonetheless, the attack rattled Corinne and the group. The decision was taken to relocate rehearsals to Bangalore, India.

In the end, only three actors from *Love's Labour's Lost* were in the cast: Nabi Tanha, Shah Mohammed and, unexpectedly, Parwin. Once the rehearsals had been moved out of Afghanistan, Parwin felt safe to join the company. It was her first chance to work since Tawab's death.

:::::

When Corinne first approached Shah Mohammed to perform in *The Comedy of Errors*, he had not been sure if he should. Since Tawab's murder, he had limited his public appearances. He mainly stayed in the studio doing voice-overs, or helping Nabi edit the short films they made for development organizations.

In truth, his discomfort had started just after that magical performance of *Love's Labour's Lost* at the Bagh-e Babur. Among the many positive reviews the production had received from all over the world, one Kabul newspaper published a report that noted, "The actors did not observe the *sharia* law, but trampled on it. They appeared on the stage half naked, chasing women." This had made Shah Mohammed deeply worried. For days he was on edge, fearing that something bad might happen to him or the other actors. Nothing did, but it had left him nervous.

"I'm not sure that I want to do any more Shakespeare in Kabul," he told Corinne who had come with the interpreter to have dinner with Shah Mohammed and his family in their home.

"No. Not in Kabul. We'll be performing in London," she said.

Shah Mohammed's eyes lit up as he looked at his wife. Soon after *Love's Labour's Lost*, their oldest daughter married and moved to London with her Afghan-born husband.

"This would give me a chance to see her after six years," he exulted.

"I didn't know you had a daughter in London," Corinne said.

"Yes, and soon I'll be a grandfather." He chuckled.

"You're too young to be a granddad!" Corinne exclaimed.

"I know, but one can't deny God's gift."

:::::

Once Shah Mohammed agreed to be in the play, he did everything he could to help Corinne find the other actors she needed. He sought out the new wave of Afghan actors who had been trained in Europe or Iran since *Love's Labour's Lost,* explaining to them what Corinne was planning and inviting them to audition.

One day, Shah Mohammed introduced Corinne to Abida Frotan, a mother, a teacher, and a new actor who worked at TOLO Television. She had appeared in a few advertisements and in small parts in movies. Corinne cast her for the one of the three female roles in *The Comedy of Errors.*

Abida had a hard time reading the text. Corinne was using a contemporary translation of *The Comedy of Errors* that had many Farsi words that Abida did not know. Shah Mohammed remembered how some of the actors in *Love's Labour's Lost* had needed extra help to master that script, so he offered to work with Abida on *The Comedy of Errors.*

"Actually, I felt obligated to assist her, because after all I was the one who had brought her into the production. I did not want the other actors to criticize me."

:::::

Nabi, predictably, had a row with Corinne during the rehearsals in India and quit the production. This time, he was given no second chances because the interpreter was no longer with the group to tame Nabi and calm Corinne; he had to go to London for business. Nabi was put on a plane to Kabul and sent home. For years after, he remained angry with Shah Mohammed for not following him. A wedge had been driven between them despite their long and close friendship.

∷∷∷

While the company was rehearsing in Bangalore, a rumor started among the actors that, because Shah Mohammed was spending so much time with Abida as she learned her lines, he was having an illicit relationship with her.

"When I first heard this, I burst out laughing," Shah Mohammed said. "I presumed one of the actors was playing an unfunny joke on me, and I thought no more about it." His mind was on the Globe Theater, where a few weeks later he had an experience every bit as amazing as the night in the emperor's garden.

"Every seat in the three levels that ringed the stage was full. Hundreds more people were standing in front of the stage. Many of them were Afghans who understood everything we were saying. In *Love's Labour's Lost*, I had been a king. Now I was playing a funny servant. I said my lines and the audience just exploded with laughter. There was so much noise in the theater I thought we were having an earthquake."

When Shah Mohammed returned to Afghanistan, the rumor that had originated in Bangalore had already spread like wildfire in Kabul. Everywhere he went, he heard people whispering about it, even his colleagues at the office. Abida was not there to help him confront the whisperers. She had stayed behind in London, where she had claimed asylum. Shah Mohammed on his own could do nothing.

"I knew I was in trouble. I didn't know how to kill the rumor. If I tried to tell people that I had only helped Abida with her lines, people would not believe me. If I stayed quiet, the rumor would spread further and wider," he lamented.

"I could not sleep, eat or work. I spent hours in the studio looking at one object for a long time, as if the desk or the chair would speak to me and tell me what to do," he recalled. He spoke as little as he could to his colleagues. He had loved all the applause and congratulations he had received in London, but how could he live with the consequences now?

One day when Shah Mohammed woke early to go to work, he saw an envelope that had been slipped under his front door. It contained a letter from the Taliban saying, "We monitor you carefully. We know you are a spy for England. We know you are making propaganda movies and clips for the infidels. We know your wife who is a teacher. We saw foreigners coming and going to your house at night. We monitor your every move. We will deal with you when we have a chance."

"I was soaked in the sweat of fear," he stated. "What could I do now? What would happen to my family if the Taliban killed me? I went back to my bedroom and lay down in my bed." His mind was filled with the images of those who had been stoned to death by the Taliban for breaking their rules.

"You look pale," his wife said. "Are you all right?"

"I'm not feeling well," he told her. "I think I'll stay home today."

"I'll leave your breakfast in the kitchen," she said, and left the room.

Shah Mohammed's wife, daughters and son went to their schools. He stayed in bed for the rest of the day, trying to think of a solution for his dilemma. He could not come up with one. The next morning he woke up and tried his best to carry on with his life as usual.

He got into his car and drove towards his office. The weather was getting dark as a strong wind had brought a heavy cloud of dust from the north. Shah Mohammed closed his car windows. He was stuck in traffic. To distract his mind from the Taliban's letter and the rumor, he turned on the radio and listened to the news. As usual, it was depressing. Some women and children had been killed in a suicide bomb attack in Helmand. Some civilians had been killed in a mosque in Kandahar when another suicide bomber had tried to kill the Governor. He tried to find a station with music, as the traffic eased and the vehicles started to move faster.

"As I turned to the left into a narrower street, my car was suddenly hit from behind by another vehicle," he said. "I knew my lights were smashed because I heard the breaking sound. I stopped and got out to confront the driver behind me. When I looked at the car that had hit mine, I saw three bearded men inside wearing turbans and looking at me in a bad way.

"I jumped back into my seat and sped away as fast as I could to get out of the area. The car behind me followed me and hit me two more times. I knew that as long as I was on that straight road, I would be chased. I turned to the left into a smaller lane and turned, then I turned to the right, then right again, and then left." The chaser lost him.

When he reached the Afghan National Television studio, he was shaking. He went to his office and did not tell anyone what had happened to him. Around four o'clock, when everyone was leaving work, he slipped out of his office and locked the door behind him.

As soon as he reached home, he told everything to his wife and children. "I must leave," he said. "They'll kill me if they find me."

"Where do you want to go?" his wife asked.

"My visa for England is still valid. It is for multiple entries."

His wife did not argue with him, and did not ask him who would take care of their children. Instead, she packed a few shirts and pants in a small suitcase. That night Shah Mohammed and his wife did not sleep. He was so concerned about his family, but his wife calmed him down as she told him that she would take care of everything.

"I want you alive," she said. "even if you have to live on another continent. If Allah wills, one day we will be one family again. But for now, your safety is the most important thing for us."

Shah Mohammed left his house with his family around nine o'clock in the morning. He stopped at one of the travel agencies in Shahr-e-Naw and bought his tickets for England. An hour later, his daughters, wife and son stood crying at the gate near the airport terminal where they had to say their goodbyes. They knew that he was doing the right thing, and that this was the only choice he had.

Three years after arriving in England, Shah Mohammed was still waiting in 2015 for the British government to accept him as a political refugee. He tried to be optimistic that his application would eventually be granted and he would one day be able to bring his family to England.

"A man who has no choice must stay optimistic," he said. "Otherwise I will die of despair."

:::::

Breshna Bahar first arrived in Paris with the production of *Sisters* in 2009. When that ended, she left for Kabul and never expected to return. Yet four years later, she was living in Paris, inching her way toward becoming a French citizen. When asked how that happened, she replied to the interpreter over Skype with a world-weary sigh, "It is a long story. If you are standing, sit. If you are sitting, lean back, for I have a lot to share." She laughed sadly in her trademark smoky voice.

"After I returned to Kabul from Paris, life was never the same. Some TV channels asked me to do interviews. I did and I talked about my experiences in France, and how much people there liked our show *Sisters*, and how they had applauded us because they had not expected Afghan woman to be so talented.

"All those interviews made people start talking about me. Unfortunately, the more people in Kabul talked about me, the more my two nephews became upset with me. I had raised them since their parents had been killed. I became their mother. Now they were twenty-two, twenty-one years old and had become the men of the house. They wanted to make the final decisions about everything. But they smoked a lot of hashish, and most of the time they were stoned.

"They complained to me that they were being called the 'bastards of Bulbul.' Sometimes our people don't understand the difference between real life and movies. I was Nabi's wife only in the TV series, *Bulbul*, not his actual wife in real life. And our relationship was professional only.

"I told them not to worry about what people are telling them.

Just carry on with their lives, because no one can stop people from talking.

"One day my nephews told me to stop acting completely. Acting is my life. They told me never to leave the house again, and that they'll provide for me. Provide by doing what? The money they were earning from dog-fighting? I thought that what they were saying to me was probably the effect of hashish, that it was making them say stupid things.

"When I was approached by Akram Barmak to make the movie *Wajma, An Afghan Love Story*, I said, 'Yes.' My daughter Wajma was in it. In fact, one of my nephews was in it, too. We had fun making it. Part of it was filmed in my house. Even my mother was in it.

"When the movie came out in 2013, it received many reviews and awards. While I was proud of my work and my daughter's success as an actress, every day my nephews were more and more insulted on the streets. People told them that I was a pimp, and my daughter, Wajma, was a prostitute, because of what they saw in the movie. [The title character, also named Wajma, gets pregnant without being married.]

"One day my nephews – whom I brought up like my own sons – tried to kill me. One of them stabbed me with a knife at the back of my neck. His knife was very sharp. My head should have dropped in front of my feet. I still don't know how I was saved. Maybe it was the angels who saved me. Maybe I had done some good deeds in the past and they became my shield.

"My sister was in our house with her children. Before my nephew struck me with his knife again, my sister stopped him. I was bleeding very badly. I held the wound with my hand as the blood was springing through my fingers. While my sister and mother stopped my nephews from attacking me again, I ran out of the house. First I drove to a private clinic where they stopped the bleeding. Then I went to the military hospital, where I got better treatment because of my work with the police.

"When I was discharged to go home, I had a nervous breakdown. I kept shouting, how could my nephews become so cruel to me? I was taken to a psychiatric hospital. I was there for two weeks. The doctors were kind to me, which helped me calm down. When I was discharged, I did not go home but to my sister's house.

"Even though I was a policewoman for twenty-four years and could put my nephews in prison – as I had put so many criminals in jail for many years – I could not bring myself to do that. A man's heart can be as hard as a stone, but a mother's heart is stiller than water and humbler than grass. Even though I did not give birth to them, I still felt motherly towards them, and I didn't want to hurt them, even after what they had done to me. So I decided to go home and talk to them, and sort things out.

"When I entered our neighborhood, people looked at me with disgust and rage in their eyes. Some people called me a whore. I had never been treated like that before. People in my neighborhood had always respected me and said hello to me. They called me 'Breshna jan.' They took pride in having a policewoman and a famous actor living among them.

"When I went inside my house, my mother was watering the flowers in the courtyard. My nephews were out. My mother was happy to see me, but she urged me to get out of the house as soon as I could. She told me that my nephews had spread a rumor about me in the neighborhood, that I was a prostitute. I could not believe my ears. How could this be possible? When other people call you a whore, a prostitute or an adulteress, that is one thing. But when your own family does that, people believe it. It was as if my nephews had released a fatwa against me, and I could not escape it. A fatwa is a fatwa.

"I took my car and drove to my office, told everything to my colleagues, and asked for their help. They were sympathetic, but said that it was a family issue and by law they could not interfere. They advised me to resolve it myself, because they could not do anything to help. They also warned me that this could be very dangerous. People could stone me to death or burn my house, and I should avoid public appearances.

"I went to my sister's house and told her everything. She suggested that I stay with her. I lived there in hiding for seven months.

The rumor got bigger and bigger. That was when I decided that my own country was no longer safe for me. Whatever I tried to do, people will still think I'm a whore. You already know what happened to Parwin's husband. I didn't want that to happen to me. I could no longer stay in my sister's house, because she was afraid for her life and her family's safety. I decided I had to get out of the country. But where could I go?

"I had another nervous breakdown. This time I could not even go to the psychiatric hospital. I was too scared. I applied for a visa to India. A week later, I was granted one, and traveled to India, where I was hospitalized in a psychiatric hospital.

"All this time, my daughter, Wajma, in France, knew what was happening to me. She talked to Ariane Mnouchkine, who very kindly sent me an invitation letter to come to France. I went to the French embassy in India, got my visa, and flew to France in 2014. I told Ariane my story. She cried with me. A few weeks later, I applied for political asylum and was granted the papers.

"I never in a hundred years thought I would be living in France," she sighed deeply. "Destiny plays its game on you whether you want it or not. The French government has been very welcoming to me and my daughter.

"Everyone dreams of living in Paris, because it is one of the most beautiful cities in the world. But in Kabul I had my own house, my car, my freedom, my fame and my authority as a policewoman. Here in Paris, I'm not in danger and the government treats me very well, but home is home." She sighed again.

"Slowly, I've been trying to make this place home. At the moment I'm learning the language. I think French is the hardest language, but now I know enough that I can solve my problems without the help of an interpreter.

"My days are long and empty. I'm thinking of studying cinema, because I never had a proper training as an actor. Maybe the professors will teach me a few things, and I may teach them a few things in return. I'm also thinking of joining the police force here in Paris. I could do both in Kabul. Why can't I do both in Paris? I don't look like a French woman, but a lot of people think I'm Greek, Italian or Spanish. When I say I'm Afghan, and I tell them what I have done in Afghanistan, they urge me to become a policewoman. I was one of the first women to appear on TV after the Taliban. Maybe I will be the first Afghan woman to be a policewoman in Paris."

:·:·:·:

Breshna's daughter, Wajma, arrived in Paris with her mother for the 2009 production of *Sisters*. With things in Afghanistan so unpredictable, she decided to stay when she was invited to join the Aftaab Theater. But she had inner doubts.

"Before I was in *Love's Labour's Lost*, I viewed acting as something that would make even a very educated person from a good family look low and cheap. Every day I saw what my mother had to go through. She is strong. I was afraid that I would not be strong enough to put up with the insults. I often dreamed of being a pilot.

"When I was rehearsing for *Love's Labour's Lost*, I dreaded the moment when I would have to stand in front of the audience and say my lines. When that time arrived, I was sweaty and shaking as I walked onto the stage. Then something I said made the crowd roar with laughter.

"Right away I was addicted to acting on the stage. I don't know how to explain it. It is like a pleasure that you can't find in anything else. You give the audience your energy, and they give you back hundred times more than what you gave them. Those weeks or months of hard work in the rehearsal room pay back in a couple of hours.

"I don't get that kind of joy from acting in front of a camera. The camera is just an object and doesn't give me anything in return. It just sucks in everything I do, whether it is good or bad.

"The problem with theater is that if you don't make it to the top in your twenties, you'd better look for other things to do in life. At the moment, I'm considering graduate programs. I'm still young. I'm only twenty-five years old. I can do it. My first choice is to study law. If I can't get into a law school, I will do literature. After three years, when I'm done, I'd like to become a professor and teach, but acting in plays will always be closest to my heart.

"For now, I have decided to stay away from Afghanistan since the situation there is not ready for people like me. After my movie *Wajma, an Afghan Love Story* came out, I received a lot of threatening emails and messages through social media. Some even from my distant family members. I have lots of things in mind to do in Afghanistan, all related to cinema and theater, but not now.

"In the meantime, here in France I will try to be in as many plays as I can. More importantly I will write my own plays, as Shakespeare did, about my country and my people both inside Afghanistan and in the Afghan diaspora."

After *Love's Labour's Lost*, Marina Golbahari continued to make movies, fifteen in all to date. She also appeared in an Afghan television series that ran for thirty episodes. Offers for new movies regularly come from directors inside and outside Afghanistan. Every day, though, she said, she feels as if she is living on the edge of danger.

Once her mobile phone vibrated in her hand. She did not recognize the number. When she pressed the green button and asked who it was, a man on the other end threatened to kill her. She turned off her phone. It was not the first time she had received such calls, or texts threatening "Stop acting or we will kill you." The next day she got a new number, but the caller somehow found her and the calls continued.

At least four times she has been caught in attacks. In 2013, she was in the northern Afghan province of Badakhshan preparing to start a new movie. After a week, though, the director decided that it was not safe enough to film. There were Taliban in the area, and he was nervous.

Everyone involved in the movie got into their cars and headed back toward Kabul. As they made their way slowly along a deeply rutted dirt road, some bearded men with guns stopped them. The men searched the cars and found the cameras. They smashed all the equipment, then started beating up the drivers. Marina was in the back seat shaking with fear, but the attackers did not recognize her and did not touch her.

After a lot of pleading by the drivers, the bearded men released them. The drivers got back into the cars and took out their rage and fear on their accelerators. As the vehicles sped southward, the passengers held tightly to the door handles or pressed their hands against the ceiling as they were thrown first one way then another by the bumpy road, all the while feeling grateful that they had not been killed.

Soon after, Marina went to Sweden for a film festival. Many cameras flashed as she stood there and smiled at the photographers. "I shook hands with hundreds of people, but I could not stop myself thinking about the attack in Badakhshan," she said. As she posed for a picture with a friendly Swedish couple, Marina decided she had to stay in Sweden. The next day, she applied for asylum.

"In Sweden, no one bothered me when I walked on the streets or strolled in the malls. No one ran to me to ask for my autograph or pestered me to take their photos with me." As the weeks passed, though, she became restless. Her years as a beggar haunted her. She thought about the movie deals she had signed before the attack, and did not want to lose the work or the income they would bring. Her family still depended on her. She felt increasingly agitated as the starting date for one of the films approached, but was not sure what to do.

After two months – during which she talked to her family for hours every day on Skype – Marina decided to go home, though many people in Sweden advised her not to.

"I want to make more movies like *Osama*, so people outside Afghanistan can understand better what Afghans are going through," she told them.

Since she had first appeared in *Osama*, she had seen how the perceptions of Afghanistan by people in other countries had changed after they watched her films. She had taken an oath to herself that for the rest of her life she would do nothing but make more movies about Afghanistan, so people everywhere could learn about her misunderstood country.

When her flight to Kabul entered Afghan air space, Marina looked out through the small window at the ragged and arid mountains below. For the first time in three months, she smiled for herself and not just for somebody's camera. She felt a sense of belonging.

"In Sweden, I had had peace, good food and very kind people who looked out for me. But I never felt I belonged there. I looked down at the sharp rocky mountains and small green valleys below and it seemed as if they all were mine."

Her mother, sisters, brothers, as well as her Uncle Barmak, were waiting for her outside the baggage claim. She cried with joy as she embraced them. She went home and told her family everything about Sweden, as she always did whenever she returned from a trip. The next day she alerted the directors who had contracted her that she was back in Kabul. One day later, she was standing in front of a camera shooting her next movie.

The rest of the year she was very busy, catching up with all she had missed. She was happy to be back and making new films. Acting was her passion, her life, and her love.

Then it happened.

One day as Marina was coming home from filming, a small group of young men on the street called her a prostitute. This was something new. She had never been insulted like that before. There is no more vicious insult for a woman in Afghanistan, or more dangerous. Women accused of prostitution are often killed. She went home and cried for the rest of the day.

At every event in which she participated outside Afghanistan, people admired her good work. Now she was in her own country, which she loved and cherished, yet some of her own people were calling her a prostitute. Why? What had she done wrong?

Marina was so heartbroken and terrified that she did not leave the house for a week. She did not want the rumor to spread. Breshna

Bahar lived only two streets away from her. Marina had witnessed what had happened to her. Perhaps if she stayed in the house, she thought, the insults and the threats they carried would go away.

Marina wondered if she had made a mistake coming back from Sweden. After a while she convinced herself that she did not have time for regrets. She resolved to put on a *burqa* whenever she left the house so people would not recognize her.

"Now everywhere I go," she said. "I cover myself with my blue cage. I hate wearing it, but what other choice do I have?"

:::::

The murder of Tawab sent a chill through Kabul's community of actors. Even those who did not know him personally respected Parwin and shared in her grief. One by one, they withdrew from public view, preferring to work behind the scenes instead of in front of an audience.

In the first few years after the play, Faisal Azizi had leading roles in several Afghan films, which gave him a following, especially among young men who responded to his swagger and his jokes. More roles were offered. After a while, though, he declined them and decided to work in an office instead.

Leila continued her education, but not her work as an actor. Even her father, who was a popular television actor and political satirist, chose to step away from the screen.

Kabir Rahimi kept his job at Afghan National Television, but stopped playing the small parts in television shows that he had been doing.

:::::

One member of the group, however, remains certain that life is good and can only get better. Daoud the driver. Since *Love's Labour's Lost*, his family has grown to five sons and one daughter. After many years as a taxi driver, he secured a permanent position as a driver and guard for the American embassy in Kabul. He still drives a taxi when the mood strikes him. Nothing makes him happier than threading his way through the clogged streets of Kabul in rush hour.

:::::

The election of Ashraf Ghani Ahmadzai as Afghanistan's president in 2014 gave many Afghans a renewed sense of hope for their country. But the unbridled optimism that had accompanied the election of Hamid Karzai ten years earlier was held in check. Afghans recognized that the peaceful transfer of power between the two presidents was a good step forward, but remained sceptical about long-term developments. They have had too many disappointments. They know that as long as the neighboring countries and larger powers around the world view Afghanistan as a chessboard for playing their strategic war games, they will have problems.

Equally debilitating are the corruption and factionalism that plague the country from within, along with attitudes born of ignorance that fail to respect the sanctity of life, especially the lives of women.

:::::

Like all Afghans, the actors are masters at living in difficult circumstances as they dream of resuming full lives in Afghanistan.

In Toronto, Parwin has focused on helping her children adjust to a new life. When they first arrived, her son, Ahmad, complained that the other boys in his school could not pronounce his name properly. He wanted to change it to Michael Jackson. Parwin eased him through his discomfort by telling him that he could not do that until they had received all their papers from the government. As time passed, Ahmad relented. "I don't want to switch my name," he told her one day. "If people can't pronounce it properly, that is their problem, not mine."

In London, Shah Mohammed settled in with his married daughter. He misses his wife and other children dearly. His eyes well up whenever he sees their photos in his wallet. He talks to them all the time on Skype. His family moved from their house in Khair Khana to a different part of Kabul after they received more threatening letters. His wife and daughters began wearing *burqas* when they go out, just to be safe. "If Allah wills," Shah Mohammad said, "one day my family will join me. Better, if Allah wills, Afghanistan will be a safe place for me to return and join my family there."

In Paris, Breshna put it as well as any: "Eventually things will calm down. People in Afghanistan are changing fast with the help of the media and the social media. Afghans are more aware of the world and their place in it than they were even a decade ago. People now defend and claim their rights, and try hard to put the greedy and bad guys in the margins. Hopefully, one day there will be more of us and fewer of the bad guys, and Afghanistan will be a stable place so that Afghans all over the world can return to our homes and breathe our own dusty air."

Insh'allah.

Glossary of Afghan Words

atan	a Pashtun warrior's dance
azan	the call to prayer
bacha ha	the boys
burqa	enveloping garment worn in public by Muslim women to protect them from the view of men and strangers
chai khana	teahouse
chapan	a long coat with sleeves of great length that dangle past the hands; often worn by the former Afghan president Hamid Karzai
hamam	a steam bath
Jumaa	Friday
Kaka	uncle
karachis	carts used by street vendors
kharijees	foreigners
kilim	a flat-woven floor covering that has no knotted pile
naan	flat bread
pakhol	flat woollen hat worn by men
patu	woollen shawl worn by men
qabuli pelau	a traditional Afghan dish made with rice garnished with raisins, pistachios, thin carrot slices and several spices, usually served with lamb or chicken
sabzi	spinach cooked with leeks
shalwar kameez	loose trousers and shirt worn in Afghanistan, Pakistan and India

shehr jangi	poetry battle
sofrah	an eating cloth
takht	a throne
toshaks	long, flat floor cushions
zikkur	Sufi religious ceremony

Acknowledgements

A Night in the Emperor's Garden would not have been possible without the cooperation of all the actors who performed *Love's Labour's Lost* in Afghanistan in 2005 and 2006. They have been generous with their time, sharing their recollections of the production in lengthy interviews that have been unsparing in their frankness.

Special thanks to Nick and Serena Jopling, whose clear-eyed understanding of what is important about this story launched this book.

Also to Dr. Irena R. Makaryk, the Vice Dean of Graduate Studies at the University of Ottawa, whose presentation on our Dari-language production of *Love's Labour's Lost* at the International Shakespeare Congress in Stratford-upon-Avon in 2008, and her scholarly article about it, published from Warsaw in 2011 in the journal *Multicultural Shakespeare: Translation, Appropriation and Performance*, first made us aware of the widespread interest in Shakespeare in Kabul.

Appreciation to Laurence E. Landrigan, Meaghan Luthin, Mai Wang and Jaqueline Mitchell for their much-valued editing, and to Christine Shields who made many helpful and needed things happen in her quiet and effective way.

Profound gratitude to Dr. Barbara Schwepcke and her team at Haus Publishing – notably Harry Hall, Aida Bahrami and Ilse Schwepcke – for their enthusiastic embrace of this book.

And an appreciation beyond our ability to express to Elspeth Cochrane who never stopped looking for ways to bring *Love's Labour's Lost* to London, and, failing that, did much to get this chronicle of its production into print.

There would have been no book if there had been no play. Thank you, British Council and the people of the United Kingdom who provided the principal funding for *Love's Labour's Lost*. Thank you, Goethe-Institut and the people of Germany who supplied additional support. Thank you, Robert Kluijver and the entire Foundation for Culture and Civil Society. Thank you, Jolyon Leslie and the Aga Khan Trust for Culture. Thank you, Shahla Nawabi for your exquisite costumes. Thank you, Qaseem Elmi for your tireless work preparing the Dari script. Thank you, Corinne Jaber, for believing it could happen despite all the challenges.

And thank you, William Shakespeare, for writing an Afghan play, even if you did not know that you had, and for giving the actors jokes that still made people laugh more than four hundred years after you wrote them.

"So now, you that way: we this way."

The Authors

Qais Akbar Omar (whose first name is pronounced "Kice") is the author of the memoir *A Fort of Nine Towers*, which has been published in over twenty languages. He has studied business at Brandeis University and earned a Master of Fine Arts degree in Creative Writing at Boston University. In 2014–15, he was a Scholar at Risk Fellow at Harvard University, where he completed his first novel, which is forthcoming. Qais has also written for the New York Times and The Atlantic. Qais serves as a goodwill ambassador for Aschiana Foundation in Kabul and for the Initiative to Educate Afghan Women. Qais was the assistant director of the 2005/6 Dari production in Kabul of *Love's Labour's Lost*. He was also the interpreter for the production's director.

Stephen Landrigan lived for six years in Kabul where he first met Qais Akbar Omar. They worked together on a project to strengthen the Afghan carpet industry, and travelled extensively in Afghanistan and neighboring countries assessing the region's carpet making. A former journalist, he has worked with The Washington Post in its London bureau and BBC Radio London from Washington. His play, *The Pan Beaters*, won London Weekend Television's Plays on Stage Award. And his staged version of *V.S. Naipaul's Miguel Street* was produced at the Edinburgh Festival Fringe before runs in London and Dublin. He helped adapt *Love's Labour's Lost* for its Kabul production and oversaw its translation into Dari.